Identity & Access Management

A Systems Engineering Approach

~2nd Edition~

Omondi Orondo, PhD

Printed in the United States of America.

Published by IAM Imprints, Boston, MA, USA.

ISBN-10: 1499357060
ISBN-13: 978-1499357066

DEDICATION

For my daughters Amisi and Odundo.

REVIEWS

"...... demonstrates a .....very useful mathematical approach towards Identity & Access Management (IAM)....... this book provides a level of generalization of IAM entities, processes and problems that enable IAM discussions in mathematical terms"

-Amazon.com

ACKNOWLEDGMENTS

I acknowledge the valuable assistance of Dr. Tamba Edward Gbondo-Tugbawa in proof reading the manuscript, and Dr. Manish Gupta for his advice during book preparation. Lastly, I would like to thank my colleagues at Acclaim Consulting Group and all our clients for their inspiration.

ABOUT THE AUTHOR

Dr. Omondi Orondo is a principal at Acclaim Consulting Group, Inc, a firm specializing in the conceptualization, architecture, design, implementation and support of Identity and Access Management (IAM) products and systems.

His other books include *A Theoretical Analysis of Interstitial Hydrogen: Pressure-Composition-Temperature, Chemical Potential Enthalpy and Entropy*, a work in the field of Engineering Physics based on his doctoral dissertation, and *The Stirring of Stagnant Time*, a fictional account of a monument to madness.

He holds a B.Sc., M.Eng. and Ph.D. degrees from the Massachusetts Institute of Technology, all in Electrical Engineering and Computer Science.

He may be reached at omondi@orondo.com.

Table of Contents

Table of Figures

Preface

This book is motivated by the realization that the current practice of Information Systems in general, and Identity and Access Management in particular, is increasingly divorced from its Systems Engineering underpinnings. Even for the most innovative and resourceful practitioners, the architecture, design, implementation and support of enterprise Information Technology systems has taken a rather complex inferential approach, driven by algorithmic and rule based protocols and standards.

Granted, the foundations of Identity and Access Management (IAM) are certainly in Computer Science and perhaps organizational management theory, but viewed as a system, the practice of IAM can greatly benefit from more than a century of Systems Engineering developments.

In this work, I attempt to create a solid foundation for IAM by using established concepts from Systems Engineering. I create systems representations for major IAM processes like authentication and authorization. Such systems formulations may then be used to analyze IAM systems in complicated organizations using established Systems Engineering methods. For example, I show that problems in IAM such as risk propagation and authentication processes that were heretofore analyzed in terms of prescriptive, algorithmic or empirical schemes, are indeed amenable to general theoretical treatment.

The main goal of this book, therefore, is to come up with the

Systems Engineering basis of Identity and Access Management within the organization.

The book acknowledges that Information Technology systems have been analyzed for a long time using automata. Mine is a different approach using basic Systems Engineering concepts. Thus my models do not, for example, replace automata theory in Computer Science in modeling authorization of users to resources.

The book is specifically designed to be accessible to the general IT practitioner. It is with this goal in mind that I tease out the concepts in a way that anyone with some college education will be able to understand. It is also likely that students of IT or Systems Engineering may find this book interesting because I have taken a novel approach to the *analysis* and *synthesis* of IAM systems.

With these goals in mind, I start by introducing aspects of enterprise IAM that are needed to demonstrate the validity my models. To create a coherent narrative, I have attempted to provide a consistent conceptual flow of fundamental ideas throughout the book, starting with a historical perspective followed by a brief tour of the IAM components and models of selected processes.

It is my belief that this work is a solid first step into our understanding of the fundamental underpinnings of IAM. I invite others to extend it.

Omondi Orondo
Boston, MA, USA, May 2014.

Preface to 2nd Edition

In this version, we have added a new chapter on modeling of Access Reviews and Certification. When we started working on the Access and Review Certification models following the background that was already laid in the first edition, it was not clear at the outset that a Systems Engineering formulation could be found. It was therefore remarkable to find out that a very solid model was accessible. We invite new and old readers to take a look at the new Chapter 4.

We have also tightened some of the existing models to make them more rigorous while still keeping the overall treatment accessible to the average IT professional. For example, in Chapter 3, we have added an alternative formulation to help us understand the Authorization models.

Last but not least, we have made some minor corrections that several readers have brought to our attention.

Omondi Orondo
Boston, MA, USA, September 2016.

Chapter 1 - Identity and Access Management

INTRODUCTION

This chapter introduces the wonderful world of Identity and Access Management to the reader. It is a summary tour of the landscape that will be covered in this book, and introduces the reader to the wide breadth of the subject.

We first briefly discuss some historical aspects of Identity and Access Management (IAM). We follow this with a brief description of the key concepts in IAM that we will continuously refer to in later chapters. We then introduce the Systems Engineering method, and relate it to IAM in a generalized manner.

Introduction to Identity and Access Management (IAM)

The need for Identity Management has been with us for a very long time. It is entirely imaginable that as soon as human beings started living in small groups, it became necessary to track where all the members of the group were. For example, it may have been a good idea to carry out a head count at the end of the day to make sure everyone was accounted for.

Perhaps another need for member tracking arose when tasks needed to be divided amongst the group's various members. Since we can presume these tasks were primarily for survival (gathering food, building shelters, fighting enemies, etc.), in a sense Identity Management ensured the very survival of the species.

There is some evidence from papyrus manuscripts that indicate that the first known effort to track human identities occurred in Babylon around 3800 BCE. These records suggest that every six or seven years, the rulers wanted an accurate count of the number of people as well as their livestock, butter, honey, milk, wool and vegetables (Statistics Canada, 2009). In Pharaonic Egypt, census was carried out around 2500 BCE to get an accurate count of the labor force needed to build the pyramids (Ibid). There was also a pre-historic census in Israel (1491 BCE) to identify those eligible for military service. In China, Confucius carried out a census in 550 BCE to establish the country's agricultural, industrial and commercial activities.

However, perhaps the earliest documented exercise in human Identity Management occurred in the Persian Empire in 500 to 499 BCE. According to records (Kuhrt, A., 1995), the Persian army wanted an accurate count of the population to determine tax rates and determine land policies.

In later periods, census was conducted primarily as a means to determine taxation levels. In India for example, Chanakya, an adviser and Prime Minister to the first Mauryan Emperor Chandragupta (c. 340-293 BC) describes an elaborate system of conducting population, economic and agricultural censuses for the purposes of taxation (Indian Census Bureau, 2009).

The Roman Empire also conducted a census of its subjects every five years, beginning with its sixth Emperor Servius Tullius (578-535 BC), and left us with an elaborate register of its citizens, complete with their property, rights and privileges. Indeed the English word 'census' is derived from the Latin 'censere' which means 'to estimate'.

In China, a census conducted in 2 AD by the Han Dynasty found 59.6 million people living in Han China (H. Yoon, 1985).

Modern censuses are not much different from these early predecessors in that they involve a count as opposed to a statistical sampling of the population. The United States, for example, carries out its census every ten years, and the exercise is indeed enshrined in its constitution (Constitution of the United States). The census is used to determine representation in Congress as well as in the Presidential Electoral College, and Federal funding of the States.

Accounting for populations and economic activity, which have been covered by many volumes elsewhere, is only one aspect of Identity Management. In this book, we are concerned with another kind of Identity Management, namely enterprise or organizational identities.

Enterprise or Organizational Identities

The identities we concern ourselves with here need to be within the context of an enterprise. The enterprise could be a business, company, governmental body or some such comparable organization.

Electronic or Non-Electronic Identities

Within an enterprise, identities may be in electronic or non-electronic form. We will develop organizing principles that cover the life cycle evolution of identities, portions of which may be in a non-electronic form during parts of the cycle.

By 'life cycle evolution', we mean exactly what might be expected in other disciplines, namely that identities have a distinct but complex path from their creation (birth), maturity and eventually destruction (deactivation or deletion). As we will see, this process is specific to an organization, but is governed by overall principles that we attempt to capture or model in a general sense, and that these organizing principles are driven by organizational processes.

Access Nexus

Our interest in Identities will be closely tied to the access that these identities have to resources within the enterprise. The resources in question may be broadly characterized as enterprise electronic properties but will mostly consist of applications and data. In other words, interesting things happen when Identities access resources, and we believe the organizing principles we espouse here will help illuminate this interaction.

Broadly defined, therefore, Identity Management is the process of managing user identities in the enterprise (Orondo, 2007). Access Management is the substrate of Identity Management as shown in the following graphic (Ibid) – see also Chapters 8-10 for a more complete treatment of Identity and Access Management (IAM) process models.

The goal of Identity Management, therefore, is to ensure that enterprise information is only accessed by those properly authorized to do so by organizational policy, as well as via applicable laws and regulations. This implies, for example, that if some medical information is deemed private, only the primary care physician will be permitted access since there are established governmental and organizational regulations that specifically allow physician access to the exclusion of others. Others may get access to the same information, but only if there is a policy or legal formulation that allows it.

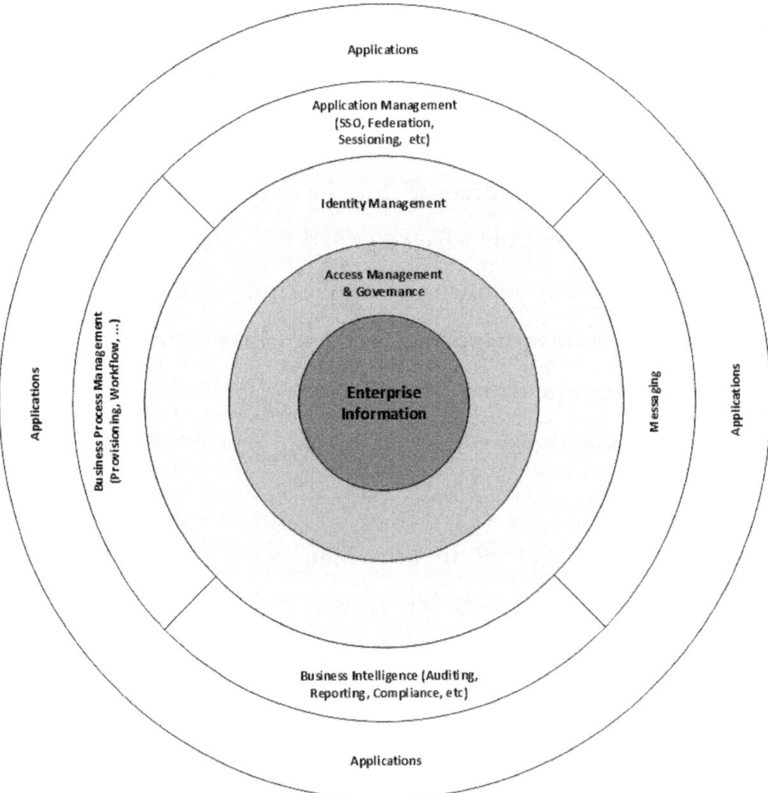

Figure 1-1: Enterprise Information Architecture: Unified IAM View

The following section discusses some of the more common themes in Identity and Access Management. It is by no means exhaustive; rather we provide only a cursory tour of the elements that we will need in later chapters. A seasoned reader may skip it without loss of continuity but we recommend it to all readers since it lays a particular view point that may not be familiar to even the seasoned professional or academic.

REVIEW OF IDENTITY AND ACCESS MANAGEMENT: THEORY & PRACTICE

There is no single unifying theory that would cover the subject of Identity and Access Management. There are however several theoretic treatments that cover different aspects of Identity and Access Management. In this sub-section, we will review them. We shall then delve into a summary of some key concepts of how IAM is practiced today. Once again, no attempt is made at full treatment. The reader is instead referred to the cited works for further information.

Access Control

The generic access control problem encountered in IAM may be described simply as follows:

A group of persons within an organization need to have access to some resources within the organization to do their work. However, there are organizational rules of internal or external origin that govern who should have access to particular resources.

In short hand,

$$\{Users\ Identities\ x_1, x_2, ..\} \rightarrow \{Business\ Rules\ \&\ Policies\ T_1, T_2, ..\} \rightarrow \{Resources\ r_1, r_2, ..\}$$

The challenge is to come up with the best way to ensure that organizational productivity (we must presume that workers (the term 'actors' may also be used) need information to do their work effectively and vice versa) is maximized while simultaneously obeying business rules and policies.

A cursory consideration of the problem may lead one to believe that this is a simple linear programming maximization problem, perhaps by feeding some program or service a set of rules and policies, together with a set of user definitions. The service then enforces access to resources at defined access points (and blocks access at all other points).

While the foregoing is clearly plausible, it is not clear that such a system could be built or even if it could, whether we can ever develop a sufficiently descriptive set of rules and policies in a generic format (as opposed to say, coding each business rule that comes up, which is evidently cumbersome to implement in practice even if it is plausible theoretically).

In 1974, Lampson introduced a framework for describing the access control problem called the Reference Monitor (Lampson, B. W., 1974). The key concept of the reference monitor is that we separate the access control decision from its enforcement.

To elaborate further on the Lampson model, we like to use the analogy of the US system of government – The Congress (Parliament in some countries) decides what the laws are and the Judicial Branch (Court System) together with the Executive Branch deal with their enforcement and dispute resolution – and some wall of separation exists between the two branches.

Similarly, the Reference Monitor model creates a wall of separation between access control mechanisms from those of enforcement. Many access control products today follow the Lampson model in their architecture since the model seems to be very intuitive. In fact the product vendors may not acknowledge or even realize that their architectures are based on this sound theory.

Another theoretical treatment of access control is the so called Confinement Problem (Lampson, B. W., 1973). The Confinement Problem is more of a rigorous formulation of the access control problem since it deals with not just user but program control as well.

Stated simply even if obliquely so, the Confinement Problem is solved when a program only provides information to its caller and no one else. In other words, the program does not leak information. Lampson proposed several rules that, when complied with, closely describes the theoretical problem of access control - presumably the program caller would pass through a reference monitor to make the framework complete:

- A confined program would make no external calls to other programs except those also confined (please note the recursive definition that ensures overall consistency in connected programs and networked applications – this definition will appeal especially to those will a pedagogic programming background).

- A confined program may not have illegitimate input or output channels.

- A confined program must comply with what it is advertised to do (This presumably removes the possibility of bugs, which may not be practical. It also excludes Trojans and other such malware)

There is also the more formal treatment of access control in computer science in terms of automata theory. See, for example, Abadi et al (Abadi, M, 1993) or Chandra et al (Chandra, A, 1981) for those adept in discrete mathematics.

Message Authenticity

In IAM, there is often a message to be passed between and amongst the Users (see below) and the Resources (programs or services) they are using. The key question is very simple, namely, how does a User (or program or service) know that the message is the same one that was sent by the Sender (another User, program or service)?

Historically, and even today, important messages have been sent by a known and trusted courier. For example, in days past, the President of the United States may have sent his Secretary of State to convey an important message in person to the Queen of England. In such a context, the message authenticity would not be in doubt, after we exclude the possibility of subterfuge on the part of the Secretary of State. If we further exclude the possibility of repudiation (and other such treachery) by either the President or the Queen, it is quite easy to guarantee the message authenticity in this scenario.

Obviously the thorny issues of treachery, subterfuge and repudiation also occur in the electronic realm. In fact, in an electronic and open, inter-connected world, there are vastly more opportunities to tamper with a message than in the analog world (or open non-connected world) where one can write a piece of information on paper and bottle it up in a brief case under constant guard. An open-connected world is one where electronic communication is conducted over public networks like the Internet (or via private networks which are themselves subject to possible tampering since portions of the network cross or inter-cross public networks).

Contrast this to an idealized closed world where electronic communication is conducted over an electronic network that is entirely and positively controlled by the communicating parties or their absolute agents.

In the electronic world, the message may be tampered with from a number of sources (attack vectors or generally, attack surface). Some of these are illustrated below without attempting to be exhaustive.

Message Confidentiality Breach

Since the communication is over a public network, an intruder may simply eavesdrop on communications between two parties. As the reader might imagine, if the communication is about war plans or trade secrets, the cost or damage from such eavesdropping may be extremely high.

Message Integrity Breach

An intruder may intercept the message en-route and substitute their message for the actual message. For the classic example, if the message was "Transfer $X from Account A to Account B", the intruder may change it to "Transfer $X from Account A to Account Z", where Account Z is controlled by the intruder. This is also often described as the "man in the middle" attack.

Message Authenticity Breach

The intruder may also completely hijack the communications and pretend to be the opposite party in the communications. A user may for example think that he is communicating with his bank, but in actuality he is communicating with an intruder. One form of this breach is the so called Phishing Attack, with its myriad variants.

Message Repudiation Breach

In a repudiation breach, a legitimate party in a communication denies that they ever participated in the communication after it has been completed. This may be advantageous to the repudiator, for example, if the results of conversation were disadvantage to her.

Message Availability Breach

The intruder may further deny legitimate users access to a program or service by tying up the service responsible for handling the communication with useless communications. This breach manifests itself in the familiar Denial of Service (DOS) attack, and its variants.

Theoretical Treatment of Message Authenticity

The most famous and enduring theoretical treatment of message authenticity was done in the field of cryptography in the 1970s by Whitfield Diffie, Martin Hellman and Ralph Merkle *(Diffie W et al, 1976)* along with Ron Rivest, Adi Shamir and Leonard Adelman *(Rivest, R., A. Shamir, L. Adleman 1978)*. Cryptography, which is the science of secrets, is bound to feature in Identity and Access Management.

There are very many published volumes and papers on cryptography. For our purposes, we provide only the briefest of sketches of some of cryptography's important elements that we need to consider in this treatment of IAM. (The reader is directed to the works cited above and others by the same authors, as well as other authors, for a more complete treatment of the subject)

The basic idea of cryptography is that the message creator hides or scrambles the message before it is sent. The hiding is done using the application of a key, very much like writing a letter and locking it in a box using a padlock before sending it to a friend.

The friend will be able to open the box and read the message only if they have the right key. Obviously, to ensure no one else can open such a box, it is necessary to restrict the identity of the keys to the communicating parties, hence the reason why the term "private key" is so prevalent in applied cryptography.

Electronic messages are similarly locked using a key that is applied to the message using a mathematical function. When the recipient wants to verify that the message actually came from the sender, they do one of two things depending on the nature of the key as discussed briefly below.

Symmetric Key

In symmetric key cryptography, the sender and the receiver mutually agree on the private key to be used ahead of time. They additionally agree on the reversible mathematical function that will be applied to the message by each party (encryption and decryption algorithms). See, for example, Delfs (Delfs et al, 2007).

The sender then applies the key and their part of the algorithm to the message before sending it. The receiver applies the reversing algorithm and key and recovers the original message.

The following is a very simple example that illustrates how symmetric key cryptography works:

§§

Agreement Before Communication:

The shared key = 2

Function (or Algorithm):

Divide shared key by 2. This is the Forward Transformed Key.

Forward-shift the position of each letter of the message by the number/ quantity of digits in the Forward Transformed Key.

Cycle back at the end of the alphabet.

Do not shift numbers, spaces or any other non-alphabetic symbols.

Reverse Function to Use:

Divide shared key by 2. This is the Reverse Transformed Key.

Shift backwards the position of each letter of the message by the Reverse Transformed Key.

Cycle backwards at the beginning of the alphabet.

Do not shift numbers, spaces or any other non-alphabetic symbols.

User A wants to send:

Let us meet for lunch @ 12PM.

User A applies the function to the message as follows:

Key = 2

Apply Function:

Divide key by 2: 2/2 = 1

Shift forward each letter position by 1:

A is position 1, B is position 2,……, Z is position 26

Becomes after forward shift

A = position 2, ….. , X = position 25, Y = position 26, Z = position 1.

New message then reads:

Mfu vt nffu gps mvodi @ 12QN.

User B receives the message:

Mfu vt nffu gps mvodi @ 12QN.

User B applies the reversing function, thus:

Divide key by 2: 2/2 = 1

Shift backward each letter position by 1:

A = position 2, ….. , X = position 25, Y = position 26, Z = position 1.

Becomes after backward shift:

A is position 1, B is position 2,……, Z is position 26

And the received message, according to this function, is

Let us meet for lunch @ 12PM.

§§

Of course in real life the function used is a lot more complicated. The intruder must be assumed to have the necessary computation power, to say, take the encrypted message and deduce what the key and encryption algorithm are, even if by brute force. Indeed, to ensure a defeat is handed to the intruder, an algorithm is chosen from a class of problems in mathematics called "Hard Problems", which are so named because their solutions are, as expected, difficult and time consuming to compute using the then current computation resources that we may assume are at the disposal of the potential intruder.

One may ask, well, how hard it "Hard"? In general, the standard used is that the mathematical function used to generate the keys may not be reverse engineered within a reasonable amount of time, using existing and even anticipated computing power. This makes symmetric key encryption somewhat of a moving target since some algorithms that are considered secure and irreversible today may not be so tomorrow as computers become more and more powerful. For a further reading on the precise computer science definition of "hard" and similar concepts, see for example Garey et al (Garey et al, 1976)

The Symmetric Key approach is used on many computer products today. Other industry terms used in conjunction with this approach to message authenticity are "shared secrets" or "symmetric key".

Note that the mathematical function itself may or may not be publicly known. Also, a number of keys may be used during the course of the communication, and some or all of these keys may be temporary. Nonetheless, the essential nature of the communication is that at any one time, the sender and the receiver share a secret key that is used to scramble messages between them.

Asymmetric Key

Asymmetric Key Cryptography is very similar to its symmetric key cousin since message authenticity is assured using a secret key. The major twist in asymmetric key cryptography is that each party in the communication has two keys. One key is secret and private while the other is public. See, for example, (Simmons, 1979).

Additionally, there is a mathematical relationship between the two keys that makes it possible for each party to keep their private key secret yet still be able to decode a message encrypted using the public key. And just like in symmetric key cryptography, it is difficult to calculate the relationship between the two keys, i.e. if all I have is the public key, it is exceedingly difficult to calculate the corresponding private key.

We will now sketch out the basic idea behind one commonly used Asymmetric Key Cryptography algorithm. It is called the RSA Algorithm (*Rivest, R., A. Shamir, L. Adleman 1978)*. It is used in everyday electronic commerce, for example, when you access your bank's online banking application or app.

Please note that this is a very rough sketch that allows us to understand the basic concepts without troubling ourselves with its underlying mathematical complexity:

(I) Take two large prime numbers, p & q:

A prime number has the property that it has no divisors except the 1 and itself. For example, 3 is a prime number because only 1 and 3 are its divisors. Other examples are 5, 7, 11, 13, etc. Note that 9 is not a prime number since 9 may be divided by divisors other than 1 and 9, namely 3.

(II) Multiply the two numbers as follows to generate another factor (number) n where: $n = p * q$.

(III) Perform another calculation (or generate the following function of n) as follows: $w(n) = (p - 1) * (q - 1)$. In this scheme, $w(n)$ is referred to as the generating function.

(IV) Choose another number, e, such that $1 < e < w(n)$, and e and $w(n)$ are relatively prime.

Two numbers are relatively prime if they share no prime factors, i.e. they have no Greatest Common Divisor (GCD – think high school math here) other than 1.

(V) Choose another number d in such a way that $d * e = 1 + k * w(n)$, i.e. the product $d * e$ is a multiple of $w(n)$ offset by one.

e above becomes the public key, while d is the private key. While this is not a work on cryptography, a vast and complicated field indeed, and understanding the above math is not integral to getting the core material in this book, the general reader with no background in cryptography or advanced mathematics may nonetheless appreciate why the RSA algorithm works:

The private key and the public key are related by the multiplication operation in step (V) above.

Now, we all learned factorization in high school, right? Since the factorization can be done in theory, it should be possible to recover the private key since we know the public key. For example

$$12 = 2 * 6$$
$$12 = 3 * 4, etc.$$

In other words, if we have the product (12) it is relatively easy to get its constituent factors. Right?

Well not quite so. It turns out that that when a number is prime and very large, this factorization is exceedingly difficult to do, even with very powerful computers. As an example, it might take several days using some of the fastest computers available (as of this writing) to carry out one of these operations. Given that your online banking session takes just a few minutes, it is easy to see why we can securely use the web for e-commerce today.

This is the essence of the RSA algorithm. The reader who needs a complete mathematical treatment may consult the works referenced above.

The above outline of the RSA algorithm ensures the following:

- If a user A intends to communicate securely with User B, then User A may apply User B's public key to a message, then send it. The only way anyone can read the message is if they applied User B's private key. Since User B's private key is kept secret by User B, only user B can read the message.

- Conversely, if User B wants to ensure that User A is who they say they are (i.e. that another person is not pretending to be User A), User B can ask User A to apply their private key to a confirmatory message. User B would then try to read the message by applying User A's public key to it. If User B can read the message, they can be sure that the message indeed came from User A. This is called *Message Signing* because in effect User A validates their authenticity by uniquely *signing* a message with the key that only they have.

IAM Service

An Identity and Access Management (IAM) Service is a user- or computer-accessible application that is under the control of the IAM System. In the business enterprise, an IAM service is usually a business application, for example, an online banking application.

In our definition of an IAM Service, we have assumed that the IAM System, which enforces identity access and management functions, exists and may not be bypassed legitimately as prescribed by the Confinement Problem model (Lampson, B. W., 1973). The IAM System therefore corresponds to Lampson's Reference Monitor, with the additional responsibilities of managing Identities.

User, Principal or Subject

Any IAM System needs to actualize its actors. In common parlance, these are the users, principals or subjects in an IAM System. In this book, we will not make a distinction between them but do acknowledge that they may mean slightly different things in other contexts – see for example (Benantar, 2006).

In IAM, a User, Principal or Subject is often, but not always or necessarily, a system representation (or abstraction) of a human being acting on the IAM System. For example, when the company accountant opens the accounting package to enter an invoice, the

IAM System will refer to her as a User named Jessica, and interact with her that way.

In a practical sense, the IAM System relies on some data store, a relational database (RDBMS) for example, as the repository of user records from which the User object (or simply the User) is built upon or from. Such a data store is called a User Store.

User Credentials

User Credentials refer to all information that the User presents to the IAM System for the purposes of verifying their own identity. These may include user name, passwords, certificates, pass phrases, tokens or some other electronic finger print.

When the IAM System prompts the user to enter their credentials, it is said to *challenge* the user.

Authentication

Authentication is the process of identifying a user to the IAM System. In its simplest form, Authentication involves two distinct sub-processes:

User Disambiguation

In this process, the IAM System locates the raw User record within the multitude of identities in its user store(s). The location may involve a search of one or more user stores since the IAM System has no fore-knowledge as to who is a legitimate User until the next step in the process (below) is complete.

User Disambiguation begins when the user accesses a secured IAM service like online banking. The IAM System detects the request as containing no security context and challenges the user to enter their Credentials.

User Authentication

In this step, the IAM System validates that a User is who they say they are through one of four major mechanisms. Each of these mechanisms is called an "Authentication Factor", and we expect more factors to be added as technology landscape changes:

Something the User Knows:

The User may present something only she knows. This is usually a password, and is really the same shared secret concept we discussed earlier under Symmetric Key Cryptography. In other words, the IAM System and the User both trust each other because each party has a shared secret, namely the password or pass phrase.

Something the User Has:

The IAM System may also validate a user's authenticity by verifying an object that the User has in their possession. In IAM terminology, the object in the user's possession is called a Token. The token is used to encapsulate a shared secret in such a way that the shared secret may not be obtained without possessing the token.

The basic premise of this authentication method is that the Token will remain in the possession of a legitimate user.

An example of a Token is a security badge that allows access to a building, or an ATM card. These cards are given to the user, and contain some form of shared secret which is verified each time the bearer presents it to the reader.

Something the User Is:

The IAM System may also verify a property that is intrinsic to the user. These include biometric information like a finger print or an iris scan that is validated against previously collected data.

Somewhere the User Is:

The IAM System may also locate the user geographically, and even calculate the velocity at which he is moving through space, and make intelligence authentication decisions based on this geospatial information.

It is important to note that User Authentication occurs *every* time the User accesses the IAM service. (The IAM Service may be a secured web site, for example, online banking) It is however customary to consider the authentication that occurs before the Security Context (see below) is created to be the "User Authentication" since this is the one that is poignantly visible to the end user. Strictly speaking, however, authentication occurs with each user request, with the only difference being that subsequent authentications are done using the already established security token.

Upon successful authentication, the IAM system issues a Security Context (below) that may be validated by other IAM services. We shall refer to all subsequent authentications as "User Validation" or "Security Context Validations".

Security Context

A Security Context is a logical representation of an authenticated user within the IAM System. In practice, the Security Context will take the form of a software Ticket or Token that indicates that the User has already been authenticated, and may contain one or more *Security Descriptors* that simply describe the nature (or attributes of) the authentication, for example, what types of credentials were presented to generate the Security Context.

The concept of a Security Context is widely used in the IAM field and is often represented in the form of an encrypted object. The reason behind its widespread use has to do with security and efficiency/usability. On the first account, it is a lot safer to authenticate the user once, i.e., the password is presented and validated once. Afterwards, a security token is created and given to the user. The user needs to present this security token each time they access a resource (since in a stateless interaction via, say, HTTP protocol, the IAM System does not know ahead of time which request has already been authenticated)

For users who present a security token, the IAM System decrypts and validates the token contents (which usually do not include any of the user's authentication factors). The process of decrypting and validating the security token also uses keys, but these are often system generated and reside entirely on the server side unlike the user password that must be passed in the clear via the IAM channel, relying only on channel or transport encryption.

A real world analogy of a Security Context occurs at the airport – before one checks-in at the perimeter security gate, they are unknown and potentially dangerous. Once a security agent checks the traveler's ID, they get a stamp indicating they are genuine and can potentially board any plane beyond the security gate. Note that the boarding agent does not usually check the travelers ID a second time, and instead trusts a security gate stamp on the boarding pass.

Authorization

Once a User is authenticated, they also need to be allowed access to enterprise resources. This process is referred to as authorization, and involves the IAM System checking its enterprise policies to ensure that the user indeed has access to the requested resource.

Just like authentication, authorization occurs during each resource request. Each authorization is done against the user's Security Context or another session specific token that relies on the Security Context.

Continuing with our airport example, the boarding pass is used by the airline to authorize a user to a particular airline and plane.

In the IAM infrastructure, User Authorization is often abstracted into a Role as described in the next section.

IAM Role

An IAM role is a system representation of what responsibilities the user is allowed to perform within the system. An IAM role usually mirrors some of the user's roles and responsibilities within the organization.

Several types of role models exist, including those of NIST (Ferraiolo et al., 2001) and that of Nyanchama and coworkers (Nyanchama & Osborn, 1999). In this work, we will concern ourselves with modeling gross features of a role, as described below, and will focus less on specific role characteristics.

The IAM System is responsible for assigning and keeping track of the user's roles for the duration of the session as well as its entire life cycle. It does this by crafting the roles based on a matrix that consists of attributes retrieved from the enterprise user repository on the one hand, and organization policies and processes on the other hand.

We will distinguish two types of roles in our consideration.

Enterprise Roles:

Enterprise IAM roles are enterprise-wide and are assigned and maintained by the Enterprise IAM system. They represent the highest abstraction of the user's function within the enterprise – for example, Jessica may be "Employee". When Jessica authenticates and authorizes, the IAM System assigns the "Employee" role to her and passes this role as a token to any enterprise applications that trust it. Another Enterprise role that is assigned to Jessica may be "Corporate Accountant".

It is easy to see that with just two enterprise roles, the IAM System has the beginnings of a framework in which to enforce enterprise policies and processes. The IAM System should for example find it quite easy to enforce the enterprise policy that stipulates that the payroll application should only be accessible to "Employees" who are also "Payroll Managers".

Application Roles:

Application Roles are used in conjunction with Enterprise Roles to provide fine grained control of business processes, usually within an application. As organizations have grown more complex and sophisticated in their use of Information Technology, the complexity of user roles has also grown in tandem. A user who is an "Employee" and "Corporate Accountant" may also be a "Corporate Account Approver", which means she is one of a few Corporate Accountants who is authorized to approve payments over a certain amount, for example.

Roles are often used in Role Based Access Control as we describe below.

Role Based Access Management (RBAM)

Enterprise and Application Roles define a user's role within the organization as we already discussed. RBAM (or sometimes RBAC – C for Control) (ibid) provides a very useful abstraction for implementing the access control problem we discussed earlier, namely:

> *A group of persons within an organization need to have access to some resources within the organization to do their work. However, there are organizational rules of internal or external origin that govern who should have access to particular resources.*

Or in short hand,

$$\{Users\ Identities\ x_1, x_2, ..\} \rightarrow \{Business\ Rules\ \&\ Policies\ T_1, T_2, ..\} \rightarrow \{Resources\ r_1, r_2, ..\} \quad \textbf{(1-1)}$$

RBAM provides a framework whereby the IAM System determines access control to a resource based on a role (Zhang et al., 2007). The IAM System may specify that the resource r_1, for example, may only be accessed by the "Employee" role. When a user tries to access Resource T_1, the IAM system only checks to see if the User has the Employee Role.

The foregoing seems like a very trivial exercise, but as we shall see later on, the RBAM framework is a very effective Access Control paradigm because it separates Role Ownership (which may change, sometimes quite often) from Access Control Policies (which are relatively more stable). For example, the Corporate Accountant Role may have different members as the organization grows or as employees move up or into the organization. However, the responsibilities of the Corporate Accountant position stay relatively stable.

RBAM also provides for a framework within which the organization may refine the definition of a role as Business Rules and Policies change with minimal impact to the IAM system. We shall discuss this in detail later.

In practice, organizations create and assign roles to users in a process called Role Mining or Role Engineering whereby manual and automated tools are used to discover a set of job functions, duties and system tasks that may be abstracted into named roles.

Identity Trust

As alluded to above, it is not always convenient for the IAM System to challenge the user each time they make a new request to an application. Instead, the user is generally challenged once, and thence on, a security token is created and used.

The concept of Identity Trust is a vast and complex subject, and may be captured by Azzedin's definition:

[Identity] Trust is the firm belief in the competence of an entity to act as expected such that this firm belief is not a fixed value associated with the entity, but rather it is subject to the entity's behavior and applies only within a specific [security] context at a given time.

(Azzedin, F, & Maheswaran, 2002), with [Identity], and [security] added to relate the definition to specific concepts here. Our nexus here is considerably simpler because we will use Azzedin's definition as applied to Internet applications (Grandison, T, Sloman, M., 2000)

Identity Trust in IAM goes through four major stages:

Identity Trust Establishment:

Identity Trust is generally established when the User supplies valid credentials. This is a fundamental stage of Identity Trust since the rest of the process relies on the true and correct Identity being established. A true and correct Identity is established when the IAM System successfully authenticates a real world actor (say Jane in Accounting).

Note that there are instances when identities do not correspond to real world actors. We will deal with these situations later on.

Identity Trust Transformation/Propagation:

After an Identity Trust is established, it has to be transformed in at least one way before it can be used within the IAM System. In a complex enterprise environment, there can be a number of such transformations, and some of which may be recursive in nature.

We will discuss the nature of such transformations in a general sense later on. For now, it is instructive to give a simple example.

§§

Example:

When a user accesses an online banking application, he may supply his credentials which typically consist of user name or account number, together with a password, and a second authentication factor. Once the user is authenticated, the IAM System typically creates a Security Context for them in the form of a client side ticket that is handed over to the user's client (e.g. browser, phone or some such device), and another server side ticket that stays within the server side IAM System.

The transformation occurs because neither of these tickets contains any Authentication Factors, yet both are used by the IAM System (and all systems that trust it) to grant access:

Step 1: Authentication

$$\begin{aligned}&\{User\ (User\ ID, Authentication\ Factors)\} \rightarrow \{IAM\ System\}\\&\rightarrow \{User\ ID', Security\ Token\ 1\}\\&\rightarrow \{User\ ID', Security\ Token\ 1\}, \{User\ ID'', Security\ Token\ 2\}, \ldots\end{aligned} \tag{1-2}$$

Step 2: Validation and Service Access

$$\{User\ ID', Security\ Token\ 1\} \rightarrow \{IAM\ System\} \rightarrow \{Access\ to\ IAM\ Service\} \tag{1-3}$$

$$\{User\ ID', Security\ Token\ 1\} \rightarrow \{Other\ IAM\ System\} \rightarrow \{Access\ to\ Other\ IAM\ Service\} \tag{1-4}$$

Note that the IAM Service may transform the supplied User ID (User ID above) into any number of other User IDs (User ID' and User ID'' above) before creating the token.

Also note that there must be a pre-existing trust relationship between the IAM System and applications or other IAM Systems in the enterprise before the Security Tokens it creates may be consumed properly.

Identity Trust Validation:

The Security Context needs to be continuously validated by the IAM System as well as by all other IAM services. The validation occurs with each request that the user makes to an application under the control or realm of the IAM System.

As we shall examine later on, Identity Trust Validation is one of the most critical aspects of the IAM System because it ensures that previously issued Security Tickets continue to be valid.

Identity Trust Termination:

Finally, once the IAM System determines that the Identity Trust has completed its lifecycle, it terminates it. The termination may be due to a number of reasons based on business rules and policies. These may range from natural expiration, expiration from inactivity or even forced expiration due to ex post facto changes in policies.

The termination of Identity Trust must also involve the termination of all trust relationships. In a relatively large enterprise, this may be challenging because some applications may still have lingering un-validated sessions.

IAM Session

The life cycle of a Security Context is referred to as an IAM Session. It begins when the user credentials are successfully validated and ends when the Identity Trust is terminated as described above.

Single Sign On

In IAM, Single Sign On (SSO) is an expression of the number of times a user has to supply their credentials when they navigate from one enterprise application to another within a single IAM Session. Single Sign On exists in an enterprise if the User only needs to supply their credentials once per IAM Session.

SSO is often seen as a convenience factor for the end user. By supplying their credentials once, the user is spared the need to continuously enter their password every time they cross an application boundary.

Conceptually, Single Sign On is relatively easy to implement. The IAM System essentially authenticates and authorizes the user then issues a Security Token. The Security Token is then passed on to applications. Since all requests pass are mediated by the IAM System, the user is not challenged for authentication even if she moves from one application to another.

When an IAM Session is terminated in an SSO environment, the process should involve the termination of multiple transformed Security Tokens, and the term *Single Logout* is often used.

In general, SSO is applicable to the Enterprise. When the User crosses the organizational boundary, they enter the realm of Federation.

Federation

Federation refers to Identity and Access Management across organizational boundaries. This most often occurs when two organizations share user identities and trust for the purposes of sharing a business application or service. When this occurs, several steps need to be completed.

First, the two firms agree on a communication protocol. This may be entirely custom, or they may use a federation standard like SAML (Security Assertions Markup Language) (Cantor et al., eds., 2005). The protocol simply defines the grammar of the communication.

Second, the two organizations agree on how their identities will be shared. One firm may decide to pass along a User ID to the other firm, which may decide to map it to a local user repository. When an Identity is passed from one organization to another, it is referred to as *federated identity*.

Finally, the two firms agree on what Security Tokens and other descriptors will be passed between them. The federation agreement may indicate which party is in charge of authenticating users (identity provider), for example, and what types of authentication factors are required. At the time of Identity Federation, the counter party (known as relying party) validates the security token to ensure that it conforms to agreement.

MODELING ENTERPRISE IDENTITY AND ACCESS MANAGEMENT SYSTEMS

In this section, we preview some of the approaches we will use to model Identity and Access Management Systems. It summarizes topics that we will delve into in more detail in later chapters. Our main goal here is to describe the framework or theory that we will adopt since we believe it provides a novel description of the enterprise. In particular, we will summarize a way of thinking about these systems for the purposes of design and analysis.

Modeling Enterprise Architecture

A generic enterprise may consist of several components: a client or user agent (such as a web browser or mobile app), a firewall component, one or several web servers, one or several IAM Systems, one or several IAM applications, and one or several stores of all types.

We depict the generic enterprise architecture as follows, Figure 1-2:

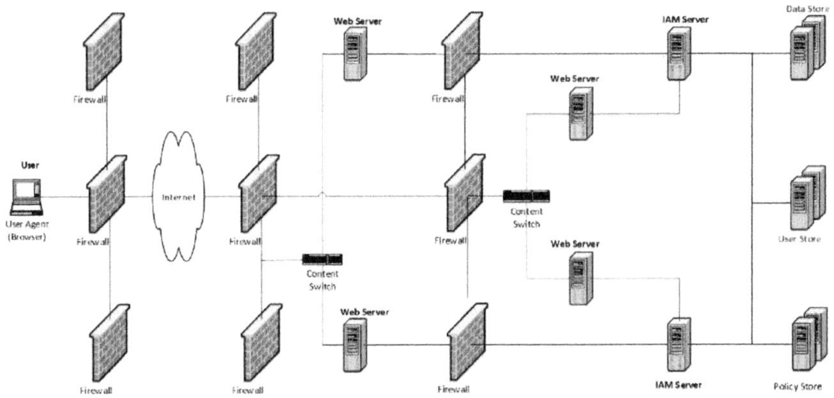

Figure 1-2: Generic Enterprise Architecture Showing Several IAM Components.

The above enterprise shows some of the common elements of an Enterprise. Functionally, it may represent a user sitting at their house, and connecting to their bank's online banking application. The user opens their *user agent*, usually an internet browser or an 'app', and accesses the bank's web site.

That request eventually makes it to the IAM Server (Reference Monitor) which in turn challenges the user for credentials as we discussed above. Upon successful authentication, the user is granted access to the online banking application if the IAM Server deems that they are duly authorized. The online banking application may also have its own access control policies, which are enforced independent of those of the IAM Server, and this may mean additional information being validated before the user actually gains access to their banking account information.

An actual enterprise will contain various components not shown in Figure 1-2 in its design; however our formulation will be general and does not assume the above architecture.

One approach to understanding the above system for the purposes of design and/or analysis, is to deal with each component's complexities. The Web Server, for example, is governed by the Hyper Text Transfer Protocol (HTTP), and it is straightforward for the most part, to design a very secure Web Server without knowing too much about the other components.

Even in situations where the architect has an enterprise-deep and -wide expertise knowledge of all the enterprise components, the thinking is still to create an overall architecture that involves the piecing together of disparate components. This process is referred to as systems integration, and an entire industry has grown around it.

Now, Figure 1-2 is indeed one model of the physical enterprise architecture. It helps us think about the physical computers, routers, servers, services, etc., by focusing on just the important aspects that we deem pertinent for the issue at hand, in this case, designing a secure enterprise IAM architecture. This is the essential definition of a model, and is not unlike building a clay (or computer) model of a bridge before building the real steel and mortar one.

Let us note that the model in Figure 1-2 is very 'physical'; in fact any enterprise practitioner can immediately visualize physical servers connected by network cables via network switches. The model mirrors the physical network layout closely. Indeed this is the very purpose of such a model, and makes it very accessible and easy to understand.

Other models of the IAM infrastructure exist.

Rather than following the network flow, as depicted in the model of Figure 1-2, we may follow another fundamental systemic theme, say, the functional process or service flow.

The following figure depicts this other view of the same enterprise architecture as in Figure 1-2 except instead of following the component or network theme, we focus on functional service flow, Figure 1-3:

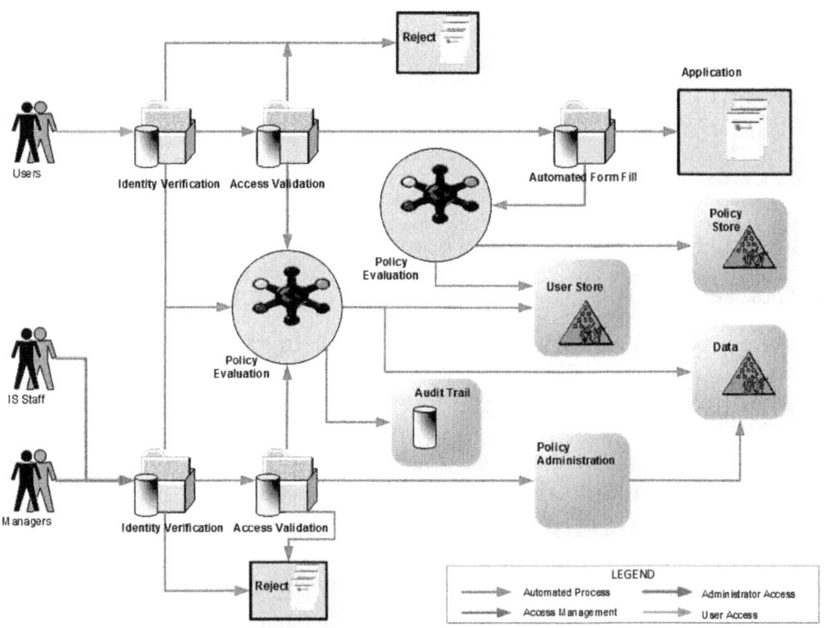

Figure 1-3: Functional Service View of a Generic Enterprise Architecture

Note that Figure 1-2 and Figure 1-3 represent the same information except they selectively emphasize some aspects while ignoring others.

In building our model, we will take advantage of such thematic translations to help us capture just the information we want for our purposes, and ignore everything else about the enterprise.

A Systems Approach

As useful as the approaches discussed in the prior section are in today's IAM enterprise, there is little doubt that their facility as design aides is rather limited. Sure, we could use Figure 1-2 as a template while designing a new IAM infrastructure. Such a template, however, will be of the most generic kind, and can provide very little aid in meeting the often rather specific organizational IAM requirements.

The functional process depicted in Figure 1-3 is even more limiting, and in fact may be used only as a guide to documenting a completed solution design since each enterprise will have a slightly or sometimes, completely different process design.

Clearly, there has to be another model or set of models that can isolate the most fundamental organizational principles that can be abstracted and used to facilitate a secure IAM infrastructure design. This is the topic for the remainder of this chapter and this book.

Systems Engineering

Systems Engineering is a very old, vast and highly complicated discipline that spans several Mathematics and Engineering disciplines. We shall not attempt to delve into any of it here, but instead refer the curious reader to one of the many introductory texts available, for example, (Siebert, 1986).

Historically, the fundamental works in System Theory were not done until the 19th century by mathematicians like J. B. Fourier (J. B. J. Fourier, 1882), Marquis Pierre Simon de LaPlace, Oliver Heaviside and others. However, some System Theory ideas were known in early Babylon according to de Santillana (de Santillana, 1961).

Systems Engineering arose primarily as a scientific endeavor to solve complex problems using the hitherto unknown analysis/synthesis approach (Siebert, 1986). In other words, to understand a complex system, we break it into its constituent components and analyze them separately. The reverse was also found to be true: to build a complex system, we synthesize it using its small constituent parts.

The fundamental idea behind Systems Engineering is that a system has an intrinsic property that transforms its inputs into some outputs.

In short hand, we can capture this relationship as follows:

$$System\ Response = System\ Function * Input\ Function \quad \textbf{(1-5)}$$

The multiplication symbol, *, is used in this sense to mean 'act on' rather than the traditional algebraic meaning (ibid).

The relationship of Equation (1-5) is not only simple but almost seems trivial. Nonetheless, it is essentially the foundation of Systems Theory and Design, whether the system is the Space Shuttle, a modern super computer or even the cell phone in your hands.

In the following chapters, we will explore and develop these Systems ideas as they relate to the IAM System.

SUMMARY

In this chapter, we have introduced the topic of Identity and Access Management to the reader. Starting from a historical perspective, we gave the reader a sense of how pervasive IAM is, and how it affects many aspects of our everyday lives.

We have also briefly summarized some of the more theoretical topics that relate to the IAM field. In particular, we briefly summarized the theoretical treatment of Access Control using a Reference Monitor, as well as the use of the Confinement Problem to model IAM systems. Our last survey of theoretical survey dealt with cryptography as a way to hide information from prying eyes.

We further surveyed the major themes, concepts, and terminologies that will be used in the rest of the book. These concepts were presented in a generic and technology neutral manner.

We then surveyed a couple of existing methods used to model Identity and Access Management Systems. We pointed out some of the strengths as well as limitations of these approaches.

Lastly, we have introduced the Systems Engineering approach, and proposed it a potential alternative framework for modeling IAM systems.

In the next chapter, we will use Systems Engineering concepts to model Identity Trust in an IAM context.

Chapter 2 - IAM Authentication System Modeling

INTRODUCTION

We will start this chapter by creating the elements of our IAM Authentication System model. These elements are the building blocks that we will use to construct our entire Authentication System Model. The elements will capture what we consider fundamental properties of the corresponding physical process.

In the process of defining the IAM Authentication System Model elements, we will create the vocabulary or semantics which will serve as shorthand of the underlying concepts. Note that the concepts are always more important than the vocabulary used to describe them.

MODELING AUTHENTICATION

We shall use the term "IAM Authenticator" to refer to an IAM service that authenticates users. As its name implies, the IAM Authenticator authenticates users to the IAM enterprise. Using a block diagram, we may represent it as follows, Figure 2-1:

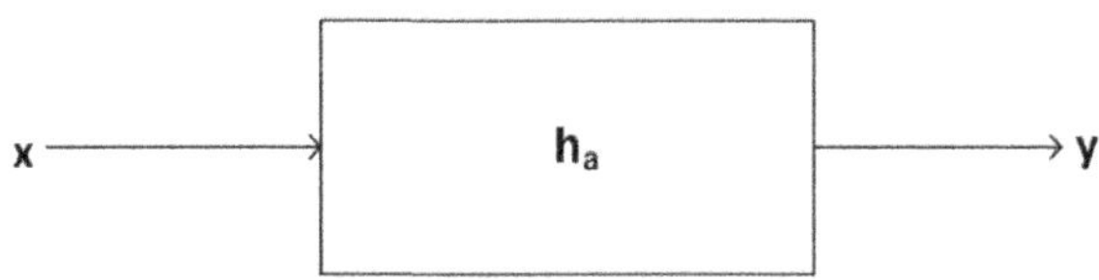

Figure 2-1: IAM Authenticator Block Diagram.

The block diagram above of an IAM Authenticator is our understanding and assignment of its fundamental behavior and properties (Figure 2-1). However complicated a real world authenticator is, we can analyze its behavior using the block diagram above, together with a corresponding systems description (or definition) of h_a, which we will characterize completely below. Obviously, we can use the same approach to synthesize (design) a system with desired characteristics.

The IAM Authenticator simply takes User ID and some credentials, or more generally, a Security Context, and returns a Boolean - *"Yes"* if the user is authenticated and returns a *"No"* otherwise. We use this fact to characterize h_a is below.

First, let us denote the Security Context using the symbol x_i. Then we can describe what the IAM Authenticator "does" as follows:

$$y = h_a * x_i \qquad \textbf{(2-1)}$$

In Equation (2-1), we have assigned the output of the IAM Authenticator the symbol y, which seems algebraic at this point.

Equation (2-1) should be read in tandem with Figure 2-1 and essentially means that y is the result of the IAM Authenticator (represented by h_a), operating on the input x_i.

It is worth noting that even though Equation (2-1) has the form of a mathematical function, we should refrain from treating it as such. Let us understand why not.

Mathematically, a function is defined as assigning an output quantity for every value of its input (also called its argument). For example, if our function is

$$y = 2x * 1 \qquad \textbf{(2-2)}$$

then, it is easy to see that for every value of the input x, the function in Equation (2-2) simply assigns an output by multiplying the input by 2 and adding 1.

Our function depicted in Equation (2-1) and Figure 2-1 may not meet this criteria, besides, in the System Engineering field, it is sometimes more useful and appropriate to use functions defined by what they do rather than what they are (Siebert, 1986).

Without straying too far from our current topic, it is important to note that functions that are defined by what they do rather than what they are have a very solid theoretical foundation in Systems Theory – they are called *distributions* or *generalized functions* (Siebert, 1986, pp. 318). The curious reader is referred to works by English Physicists Paul Dirac(Dirac, P., 1958) and Oliver Heaviside (Heaviside, O., 1892) and (Heaviside, O., 1893), who provided the theoretical foundations of generalized functions and introduced their widespread use and acceptance in Systems Engineering (Siebert, 1986, pp. 319).

Now that we understand the context of Equation (2-1), we can continue on our quest to complete the definition of h_a.

§§

From a practical perspective, something called "an Authenticator" might return a Boolean - *"Yes"* if the user is authenticated and *"No"* if they are not. We may represent this as follows:

$$y = h_a * x_i = \begin{cases} 1 \; if \; user \; is \; authenticated \\ 0 \; if \; user \; is \; not \; authenticated \end{cases} \qquad \textbf{(2-3)}$$

In Equation (2-3), we have used *"1"* to signify that the user was authenticated and *"0"* to signify that the user was not authenticated.

The last hurdle in our endeavor to completely characterize the IAM Authenticator is to define what it means *"if the user is authenticated"* and *"if the user is not authenticated"* within the context of an enterprise, for even though the abstract Boolean is well understood in logic, we need to provide a context specific interpretation. This will allow us to eliminate any analytical difficulty in evaluating Equation (2-3).

In an IAM System, the user is authenticated using some form of an authentication source. Such a source may be a User Directory as depicted in Figure 2-1. The actual authentication may be accomplished, for example, by the IAM System presenting the User Credentials to the User Directory, whereas the User Directory returns a Boolean - *"Yes"* if the supplied User ID and Credentials match or *"No"* if they don't.

Furthermore, as we saw in Chapter 1, the user is actually continuously authenticated with every request, with the later "authentications" being generally referred to as "User Validations" or "Security Context Validations". We are not concerned with the mechanics of this validation yet, but for the purposes of our present model, it is instructive to note that in either case some store with a possibly encrypted, predefined value is used to check a token that the user has supplied – or some cryptographic function is performed on the token, with an expected known value. The curious reader is referred to many books on the mechanics of authentication using current technologies, for example, (Todorov, 2007).

From a Systems point of view, therefore, User Authentication and User Validation are essentially equivalent.

We can make further progress by modeling the authentication source, which we do next.

MODELING AUTHENTICATION SOURCE

We shall refer to an authentication source as an IAM Credentials Validator. It takes a Security Context and returns a Boolean *Yes* or a *No* depending on whether the Security Context is valid or not. The Validator has a store of necessary information, and that is where we begin our model.

We may think of the credentials store as consisting of User ID and Password pairs or, more generally, pairs of User Identifier, I_n, and some Security Token, S_n. If we call such credentials C_n, then we may use the following representation for the credentials store:

$$C_n = \{I_n, S_n\} \qquad \textbf{(2-4)}$$

We visualize the Credentials for the User I_n being found at the nth location in the data store, which we may be an array or database table or some other similar storage mechanism. In Systems terms, we may also represent the credentials store visually as follows, Figure 2-2:

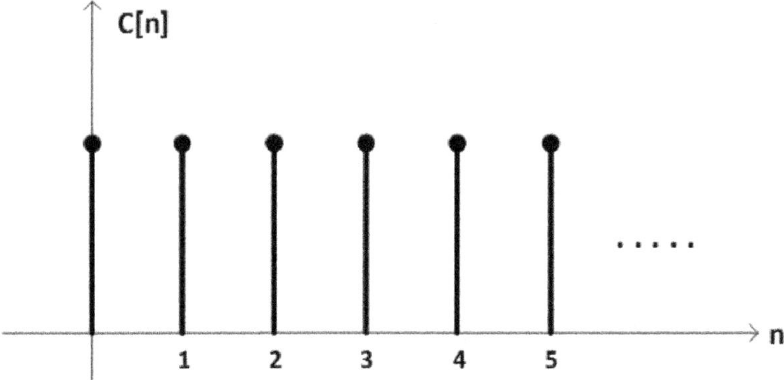

Figure 2-2: Systems Representation of Stored User Credentials.

Note that other storage schemes, for example a tree-like structure like LDAP may be similarly visualized after slight conceptual modifications. Our particular linear representation does not therefore impose any limitations on the model.

We see that our representation of the credentials is discrete; this makes intuitive sense since the credentials are expected to be discrete by nature for the most part. Even 'continuous authentication' systems like risk based authentication methods crystallize their results in terms of one or more risk scores which may be quantized into discrete values.

Also note further that we have chosen n as an index for convenience. By way of an example, if the User Jessica's credentials are stored at position number 4 in Figure 2-2, then,

$$C_{Jessica} = C_4 = \{I_4, S_4\} \quad \textbf{(2-5)}$$

and this is represented by the 5th bar, since our index starts at zero.

If Jessica did not have a password, or there was some problem with her password, the position number 4 will still be used to represent Jessica, but the length of the bar may be zero, for example, Figure 2-3:

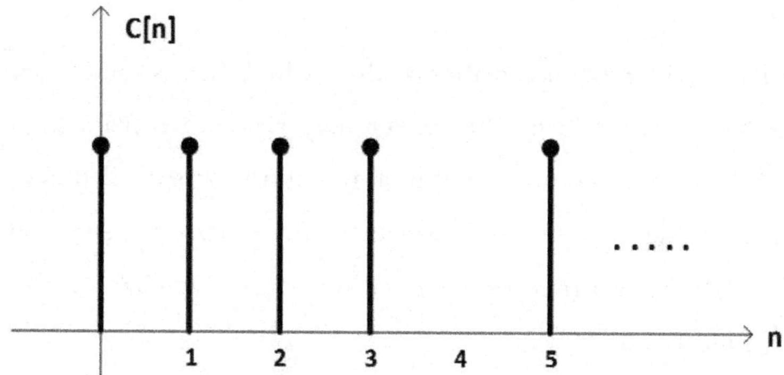

Figure 2-3: Systems Representation of Stored User Credentials (Example)

For the model of our authentication source to be complete, we need to take into account the fact that each stored credential is different from the other – recall that each nth point in Figure 2-2 above represents a User ID and its corresponding credentials. Because each User ID and Credentials combination is different and unique, we need to take this into account in our model (or else someone may be able to authenticate as another person, in which case our model would be entirely defective).

§§

There are several elementary theoretical devices that we may use to accomplish User ID and Credentials combination uniqueness. One simple one is to represent each credential in Figure 2-2 as a vector in orthogonal N-dimensional space, where N represents the total number of objects in the User or Credentials Store, in which case Figure 2-2 may be taken to represent the magnitude of such vector.

To clarify the idea behind orthogonality, which may sound more complicated than it really is, the reader may remember from high school algebra that a vector is simply a geometric or spatial object that has magnitude (length) and direction, θ. In two dimensional space, this is all the information we need to completely characterize the vector, Figure 2-4:

Note that the example vector above is at some angle θ off the x-axis, and has a component on both dimensions. Using this information, we may represent this vector as a sum of its two components, one along the x-axis and another along the y-axis, Equation (2-6):

$$\vec{v} = \vec{x}\cos\theta + \vec{y}\sin\theta \qquad \textbf{(2-6)}$$

Still in this two dimensional space, we may come up with two vectors that have their components entirely on one dimension (axis) or the other. These two vectors are perpendicular to each other and are said to be *orthogonal*. We depict them in Figure 2-5:

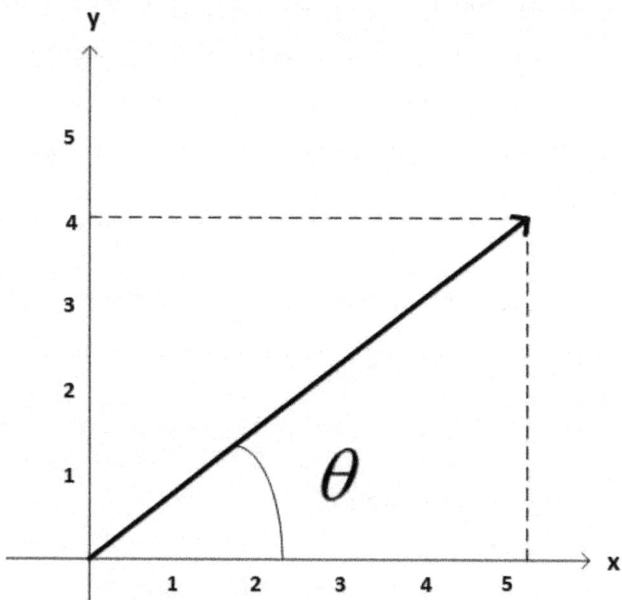

Figure 2-4: Example Vector in Two Dimensional Space.

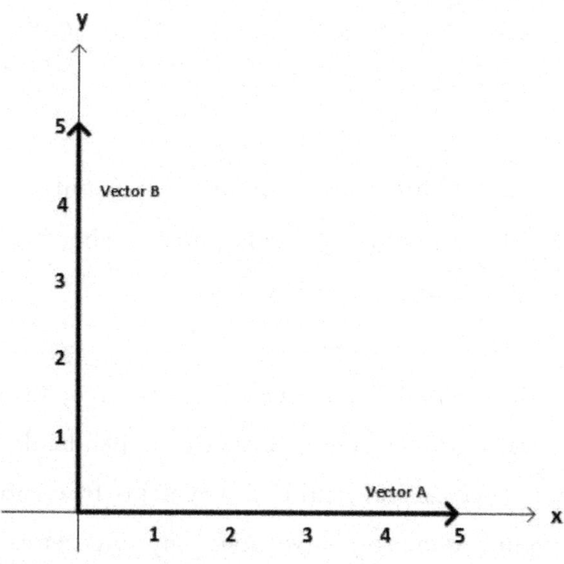

Figure 2-5: Orthogonal Vectors in Two Dimensions.

The two vectors shown above, Figure 2-5, are perpendicular to each other, and in two dimensions, perpendicularity signifies orthogonality, and essentially means Vector A above has no component in Vector B, and vice versa. We can see this very easily in two dimensions, Figure 2-5.

Using Equation (2-6) with $\theta = 0$ for Vector A and $\theta = 90^0$ for Vector B, together with elementary algebra, we get, Equations (2-7) and (2-8):

$$\begin{aligned} \vec{v}_A &= \vec{x}\cos\theta + \vec{y}\sin\theta \\ &= 5\vec{x} \end{aligned} \tag{2-7}$$

and

$$\begin{aligned} \vec{v}_B &= \vec{x}\cos\theta + \vec{y}\sin\theta \\ &= 5\vec{y} \end{aligned} \tag{2-8}$$

Equations (2-7) and (2-8) show that Vector A has only $\vec{x}$ component and Vector B has only $\bar{y}$ component. They are orthogonal (or simply perpendicular).

We may extend the idea behind Equations (2-7) and (2-8) into higher dimensions. We can easily imagine similarly perpendicular vectors in 3 dimensional space, however, the idea remains true and indeed translates to higher dimensions without any theoretical difficulty, even if we cannot visualize dimensions greater than three:

If we choose the number of dimensions as N, the same as the total number of credentials stored in our Credentials Store, then we can guarantee that our credentials will be unique if each is represented by a vector in an N-dimensional orthogonal space.

Note that our orthogonal formulation of the authentication source guarantees that there will be no password collisions for example, a property that anyone would want in their Credentials Store.

In terms of representation, therefore, we may modify User Credentials store representation of Figure 2-2 in such a way that each discrete point represents a vector in N-dimensions. Each such vector (even in N-Dimensions) is completely characterized by a magnitude and an angle, where the angle is now an N-dimensional angle.

For brevity, we will use the following two dimensional visual representation, which may be thought of as representing the magnitude of each such vector, Figure 2-6:

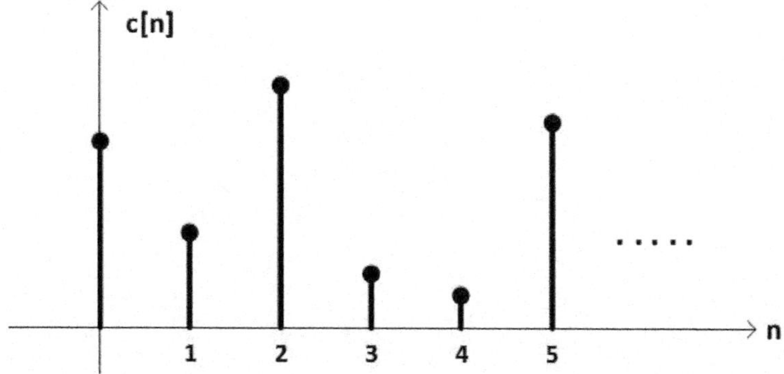

Figure 2-6: Sample Credentials Store Representation in N-Dimensional Orthogonal Space.

Our representation guarantees unique user credentials, but it is not necessary to have the dimension equal to N. We can achieve the same uniqueness with a lower dimension if we, for example, drop the orthogonality requirement, but arrange to store the credentials at different angular locations within a fixed dimension. Using this scheme, we would presumably need to keep track of where each credential is stored.

We will use the above formulation in what follows since it makes the formulation simpler, but with the caveat that it is not a necessary part of the model.

USER CREDENTIALS MODELING

For the IAM Validator to behave like its real life counter-part, we will introduce the Unit Sample Function to help us capture the model of the supplied user credentials.

Unit Sample Function

The Unit Sample Function has great theoretical significance in Systems Engineering. It is also a generalized function in the sense already discussed above (Heaviside, O., 1892).

The Unit Sample Function is defined as follows, Equation (2-9):

$$\delta[n] = \begin{cases} 1, n = 0 \\ 0, n \neq 0 \end{cases} \tag{2-9}$$

The Unit Sample Function is easiest visualized as a single unit sample at $n = 0$. Mirroring our treatment of the systems representation of user credentials stored in a data store (Figure 2-2), we can easily visualize what the Unit Sample Function is, Figure 2-7:

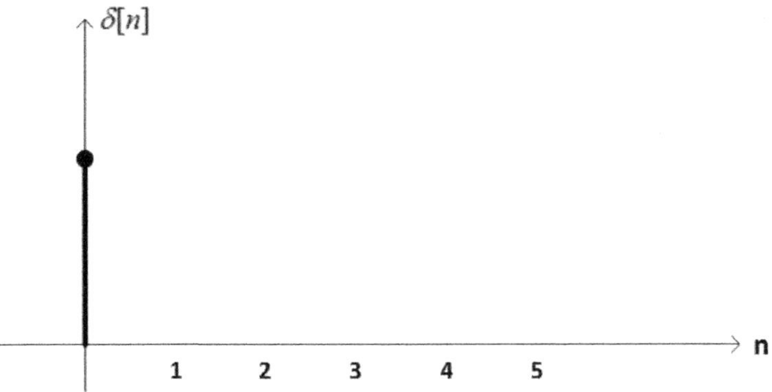

Figure 2-7: Unit Sample Function.

Figure 2-7 shows a Unit Sample Function at the origin ($n = 0$). We can surely imagine the function being at some other value of n. If that were the case, we may have the Unit Sample Function shown below, Figure 2-8:

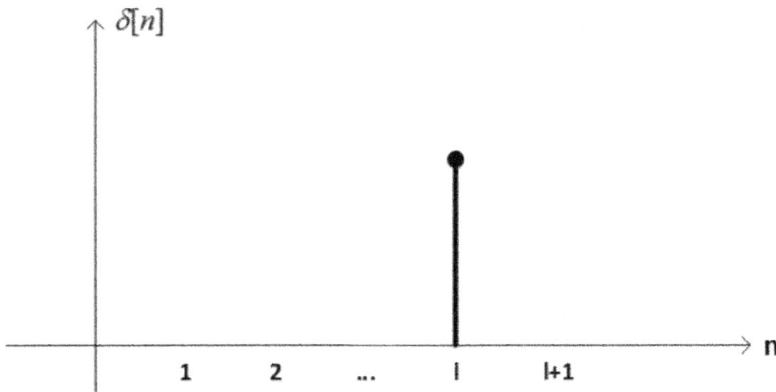

Figure 2-8: Unit Sample Function at $n = l$.

In the example of Figure 2-8, we have shown an example of a Unit Sample Function that occurs at some $n = l$. It is represented using the following expression which is very similar to Equation (2-9):

$$\delta[n-l] = \begin{cases} 1, n = l \\ 0, n \neq l \end{cases} \tag{2-10}$$

Note that the Unit Sample is also called the Discrete Unit Impulse function, and is an extremely useful analysis tool as we shall see shortly.

By way of an example, we may be able to use the Unit Sample Function as a building block of any arbitrary discrete function. For example the function shown in Figure 2-2 above may be represented by using the Unit Sample Function.

Let's see how this might be done.

§§

If $x[n]$ is some arbitrary discrete function of n similar to our model of user credentials of Figure 2-6, each point of which, we may recall, represents the user credentials as a vector in N dimensions, then we can express it as,

$$x[n] = x[0]\delta[n] + x[1]\delta[n-1] + x[2]\delta[n-2] + \cdots \quad \textbf{(2-11)}$$

or

$$x[n] = \sum_{m=0}^{m=N} x[m]\delta[n-m] \quad \textbf{(2-12)}$$

where N may represent some physical limit of the data we are dealing with. In the case of User Credentials, N is the size of the User Store or size of the Security Token cache.

We interpret Equation (2-11) as synthesizing $x[n]$ – each term in this equation contains the Unit Sample Function which, from Equation (2-10) is non-zero at exactly one location (where its argument is zero). For example, using Equation (2-11), we may compute $x[2]$ as follows:

By simple substitution of $n = 2$, we get:

$$x[2] = x[0]\delta[2] + x[1]\delta[2-1] + x[2]\delta[2-2] + \cdots \quad \textbf{(2-13)}$$

Note that all the terms on the right vanish except $x[2]\delta[2-2]$

since the Unit Sample Function is only nonzero when its argument is zero according to Equation (2-10) and Figure 2-7.

Therefore:

$$x[2] = x[2] \tag{2-14}$$

which is indeed true, i.e. we have reproduced the original function faithfully using the unit sample function (after completing the above exercise for other values of n other than 2, according to the summation of Equation (2-12))

Also note from Equation (2-12) that since $x[n]$ is a function of the subscript n, we have performed our addition over another arbitrary index, m.

If we apply Equation (2-12) to Equation (2-10), and noting that an arbitrary user's credentials will contain some vector information very similar to that discussed in relation to the Credentials Store, it may be represented as follows, Equation (2-15):

$$\vec{x}[n] = \vec{a}_i \delta[n - l] \tag{2-15}$$

In Equation (2-15), $\vec{a}_i$ is a vector in N dimensions, the same dimension as the Credentials Store. We note that a user like Jessica will present only one piece of credentials (or at the very least she will present them one at a time). We have assigned it position $n = l$ which is also arbitrary.

Further note that Equation (2-15) represents the user's credentials as a weighted Unit Sample at some position $n = l$ indexed against the User Credentials Store. In other words, Equation (2-15) is nothing more than a re-casting of Jessica's credentials as visualized below (but note that we are representing the magnitude of a vector in N dimensions), Figure 2-9:

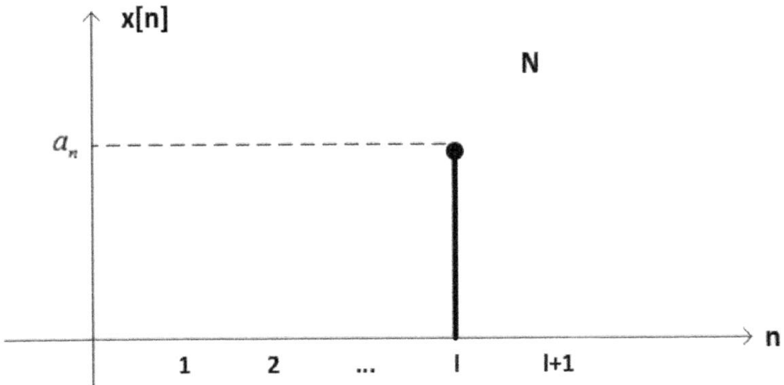

Figure 2-9: User Credentials Representation Using a Unit Sample Function.

We shall see shortly why this recasting is useful.

Last but not least, we note that the Credentials Store representation (Figure 2-2) has a very similar form to our Unit Sample Function. In fact, if we take the unit sample function, shift it to the right and replicate each shifted position pieces N times, each time assigning the appropriate weight at every location, we end up with the Credentials Store. We denote it as follows, in much the same manner as Equation (2-15):

$$\vec{c}[n] = \sum_{m=0}^{m=N} \vec{b}_n c[m]\delta[n-m] \qquad \textbf{(2-16)}$$

In Equation (2-16), $\vec{b}_n$ is a vector in N dimensions that represents the stored credentials at the nth location.

COMPLETING THE AUTHENTICATION MODEL

To complete the model of authentication, we have to bring together both the Authentication Source and Credential elements above. From a practical point of view, it is obvious that the following must be true for our model to be consistent with an IAM Authenticator as we have defined it above:

- The overall behavior of the entire authentication process is captured by Equation (2-1), which we now recast into the arbitrary discrete space, n, while retaining our N dimensional vector representation of both stored and presented user credentials:

$$y[n] = \vec{h}_a[n] * \vec{x}_i[n] \tag{2-17}$$

- For the authentication model to behave properly and match its real life IAM Systems counterpart such that Equation (2-3) must be true, i.e. the authentication service must return a *1* or *True* if the user is authentication and a *0* or *False* if they are not. We recast Equation (2-3) in the discrete space n as follows:

$$y[n] = \vec{h}_a[n] * \vec{x}_i[n] = \begin{cases} 1 \; if \; user \; is \; authenticated \\ 0 \; if \; user \; is \; not \; authenticated \end{cases} \tag{2-18}$$

- The Credentials Store or Authentication Source is represented by Equation (2-16), which we copy below:

$$\vec{c}[n] = \sum_{m=0}^{m=N} \vec{b}_n c[m]\delta[n-m] \qquad \textbf{(2-19)}$$

- The User Credentials are modeled as a modified or weighted Unit Sample function at some arbitrary position l, Equation (2-15):

$$\vec{x}[n] = \vec{a}_i \delta[n-l] \qquad \textbf{(2-20)}$$

The process of Authentication, from a systems perspective, therefore, involves simply 'picking out' or 'selecting' the correct credentials value, supplied by the user and indicated in Equation (2-20), among all the possible values in the Credentials Store, indicated by Equation (2-19).

From an empirical algorithmic or IT implementation perspective, accomplishing the last step is straightforward: simply perform a database or similar table or tree search, compare, then return 1 ("True") or 0 ("False") according to whether there is a match or not.

From a Systems Engineering perspective, things are a little bit different and perhaps more interesting. Additionally, at first glance at least, things are not as simple either.

To illustrate how the last step may be achieved analytically, we can use the following visual aide:

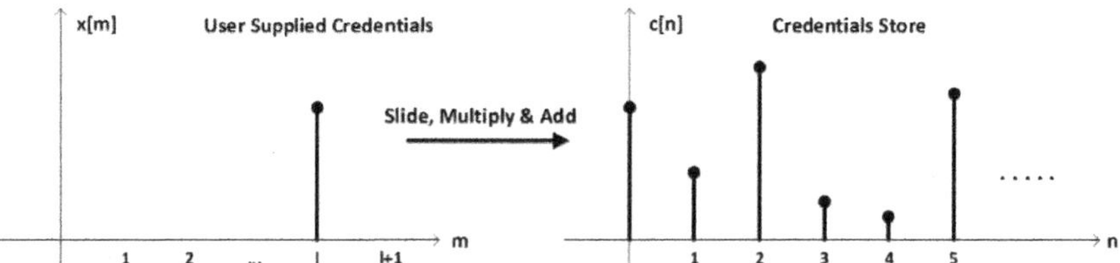

Figure 2-10: Visual Representation of an IAM System Authentication Process

- On the left is the User Credentials model from Figure 2-9. We have changed the discrete counter from n to m to distinguish its counter from that of the Credentials Store.

- On the right is the model of the Credentials Store that we are using as reference (Figure 2-6). The supplied credentials may exist at some arbitrary position, say i, in the Credentials Store, or they may exist at the same i^{th} position, but with some defect (say the password has expired), or they may not exist at all, amongst other possibilities.

- To detect whether the supplied User Credentials exist in the Credentials Store, we will conceptually slide a flipped/rotated supplied credentials into the store (this process, alas, may also match the physical process of searching for the user in the user store). The flipping/rotation of the supplied credentials is necessary to ensure that our starting point for the addition, $n = 0$, does not contain any overlap. At each position, we multiply the two functions at each overlap point, then sum the total overlap to get a single point in the output $y[n]$. The points of overlap are defined as those points whereby both $x[m]$ and $c[n]$ are non-zero, whereupon we simply calculate the vector 'dot' product of the two.

- If we further remember that the stored credentials space is orthogonal, it is perhaps easy to see that our "slide, multiply and add" process will at once yield a non-zero result only when the user supplied credentials are found in the Credentials Store.

- Typically, authentication proceeds in two steps - see the discussion in Chapter 1, *Authentication* section. In the first step, the IAM System identifies the user. The second step is the actual user authentication that we model here. With proper representation of the user identity, I_n, we may use the same methodology to model user disambiguation in system engineering terms.

  - ✓ Note: We have used the basic algebraic result that a multiplication of orthogonal vectors always results in zero.

  - ✓ The input credentials are assumed to have the same representation in N dimensional space equivalent to the one stored in the Credentials Store even though this assumption is not necessary since the IAM

System may perform the necessary transformation on the user supplied credentials to make the two consistent.

✓ As mentioned above, orthogonality is not a necessary condition, but a simplifying assumption.

In equation form, Figure 2-10 may be expressed as follows, Equation (2-21):

$$y[n] = \sum_{m=0}^{m=n} \vec{x}[n-m] * \vec{c}[m] \qquad \textbf{(2-21)}$$

Note that the following mathematical treatment of Equation (2-21) et seq. may be skipped without loss of continuity as long as the reader understands the visual explanation above.

§§

Some readers may recognize Equation (2-21) as the discrete space convolution of the input credentials with the stored credentials. From a Systems Engineering perspective, therefore, Authentication is simply the convolution of the user's supplied credentials with the Credentials Store.

Keeping in mind the orthogonality assumption we made with respect to stored credentials, Equation (2-21) and Figure 2-10, we may carry out the convolution to yield another unit sample representing $y[n]$ *– all convolution sums disappear except at the location where the correct stored credentials matching the supplied one is found, i.e.* $y[n]$ *and* $x[n]$ *look identical to each other in representation except perhaps in amplitude (Figure 2-11)*

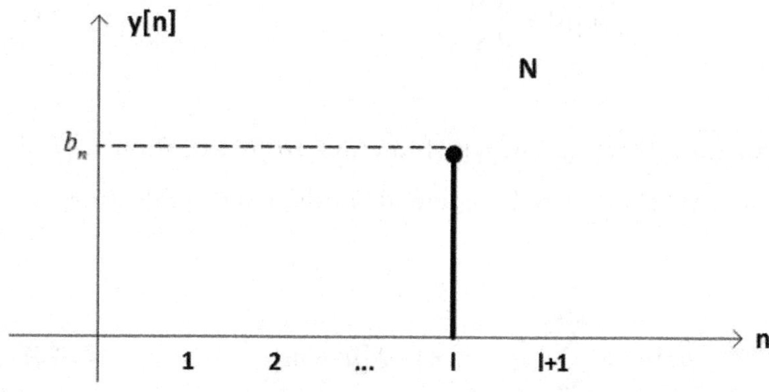

Figure 2-11: Representation of a Convolution/Authentication Result.

Substituting $\vec{x}[n]$ from Equation (2-20) (set $n = l$ since the user credentials are by definition assumed to be located at position l), and $\vec{c}[n]$ from Equation (2-19) into Equation (2-21), we get:

$$y[n] = \sum_{m=0}^{m=n} \vec{a}_l * \vec{b}_n * \delta[l-m] * \delta[m] \quad \textbf{(2-22)}$$

Even without evaluating Equation (2-22), we can immediately see that if the user supplied the correct credentials, all the terms will be zero except at the index where the correct credentials match is found. If we call this index *l*, and normalize the product of $\vec{a}_l * \vec{b}_n$, i.e.

$$\vec{a}_l * \vec{b}_n = 1 \quad \textbf{(2-23)}$$

then we will indeed get the desired analytical and correct result that we set out to find, namely:

$$y[n] = \begin{cases} 1, n = l \\ 0, n \neq l \end{cases} \quad \textbf{(2-24)}$$

We also note that our System Function from Equation (2-1) is nothing more that the stored credentials in the Credentials Store:

$$\vec{h}_a[n] = \sum_{m=0}^{m=N} \vec{b}_l * c[m] * \delta[n-m] \quad \textbf{(2-25)}$$

The interesting result here is that our authentication process has a well-established theoretical representation in Systems Engineering: convolution.

SUMMARY

In this chapter, we have created a simple analytical model of the IAM Authentication process. We began by modeling the entire process using a generic system function which we postulated must describe the physical process.

We then used generalized functions to describe the behavior of each component of the authentication process. The key result is that, from a Systems Engineering perspective, user authentication is equivalent to discrete space convolution of the supplied user credentials and user credentials store, each properly modeled. Furthermore, we have shown using basic examples that the process of authentication is thus faithfully represented in our model.

Chapter 3 - IAM Authorization Modeling

INTRODUCTION

In Chapter 2, we created a model for User Authentication. We reached the analytical conclusion that authentication process may be represented in Systems Engineering terms by a convolution in discrete space of the user supplied credentials with the stored ones from the user store.

This chapter deals with authorization, which, as we saw earlier, involves allowing users to optimally access enterprise resources. From a practical point of view, the means and methods of authorization will vary widely from one organization to another even if their authentication model is relatively similar.

Several factors go into IAM Authorization, some of which are already summarized above.

Government Regulations often mandate data protection policies, processes and standards. Regulations like HIPAA, for example, set specific rules regarding patient information protection that directly affect how organizations design and implement their authorization regimes.

Above all, however, organizational IAM Authorization complexity is affected by the nature of the organization and its business processes; in other words, what makes this organization different and unique from all others.

Last but not least, IAM Authorization also tends to be more dynamic since organizations are constantly tweaking their business models, and some of these tweaks inevitably end up filtering down to the way users are authorized within the enterprise.

Based on this brief introduction, we expect IAM authorization to be very interesting to model in System Engineering terms. Additionally, we would expect Systems thinking to provide, hopefully, a clarifying note to an inherently complex cacophony.

THINKING ABOUT IAM AUTHORIZATION

Before we bring Systems Engineering to bear onto the topic, it may be useful to spend a few moments to step back and think about the problem in general terms.

First of all, as briefly mentioned above, the biggest driver of IAM authorization is business processes (or business requirements) that are often unique to an organization. We however cannot create a model specific to an organization, for in that case our model would not be of much use. One of our goals here, therefore, is to come up with ways of describing organization processes or business requirements, in general terms, as sources of authorization information.

We will also utilize Roles, specifically Roles Based Access Management (RBAM), which, as pointed out in (Orondo, 2007), creates an abstraction layer between application authorization management on the one hand and business requirements, organizational standards and policies on the other. From this perspective, a "Role" is a logical construct that represents the organizational, governmental or other policy governing a principal's resource, application or service privileges. In other words, RBAM is another component that we need to understand and model.

Third, we have also briefly discussed governmental regulations, industry standards or some such mandates as they impact on the authorization process. From a Systems perspective, we will be asking ourselves if a government mandate is any different from a business requirement, policy or standard. If not, we will lump the two together for the purposes of analysis; if they are indeed different, we will model them separately.

Finally, there are resources that the user was trying to get to in the first place. We need to model these effectively as well.

With the big picture in place, we get the following visual representation.

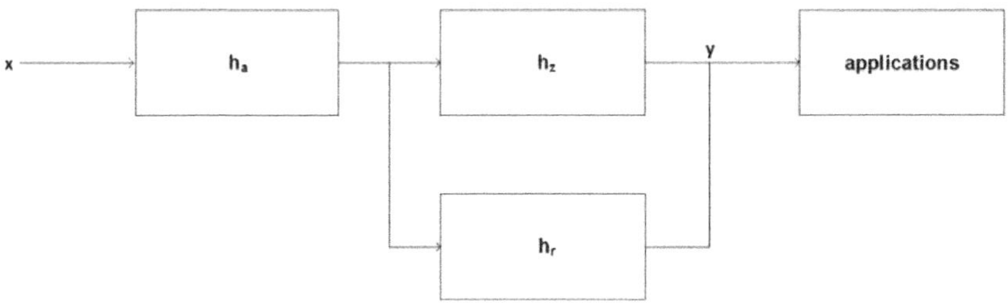

Figure 3-1: High Level Authorization Representation

In Figure 3-1, a generic user x authenticates according to the model in Chapter 2, represented by h_a. After they are authenticated, the IAM System takes them through the authorization system, represented by h_z and h_r.

h_z represents the organization's business policies, standard, processes and requirements while h_r represents effects of regulatory or industry compliance on authorization. y represents the output of the entire process, i.e. a user who is either authenticated and authorized or one who is authenticated but not authorized to view a particular resource.

We may refer to y as an *assertion* as long as long as we keep in mind that it is intimately tied to a User ID, i.e. an authorization is a function of a user (or applies to a specific user):

$$y \rightarrow y(x) \qquad \textbf{(3-1)}$$

Note:
The general idea of an assertion is similar across several different contexts:

In the common English language usage, an assertion is a positive statement or declaration, often without support or reason.

In the field of Computer Science, an assertion is a true-false statement. Assertions are often used in computer programs to state the programmer's expectations regarding program execution – and often used to check program correctness, see for example, Hoare, C., 1969.

In the context of Identity and Access Management, assertions are most often associated with Identity Federation, specifically the Security Markup Assertions Language (SAML), the XML-based protocol for exchanging security information between distinct organizations (Cantor et al., eds., 2005). A SAML Assertion is thus a collection of statements made by the Identifying Party (or Identity Provider) that vouches for the user, for example, stating that the user has already authenticated with specified authentication factors, and/or what attributes they are associated with.

In the context of Equation (3-1), an assertion is more in line with a

SAML assertion even though in what follows we will not restrict ourselves to the specific meaning implied by SAML federation (ibid), but instead apply it to any generic IAM Identifying Party.

An authorization is used by the applications to automatically grant access to the user it refers to since the assertion $y(x)$ also contains the information about the resource (see below).

Note that we have not made any assumptions about the nature of authorization other than to assume that authorization will be affected mostly by internal business requirements and organizational policies, processes and standards, as well as regulatory and industry mandates.

Also note that we have not represented RBAM at all in Figure 3-1; however from a Systems perspective, RBAM will certainly affect how we formulate h_z and h_r. We tackle these models next.

A Simplifying Assumption

The first simplifying assumption we will make to our generic authorization representation in Figure 3-1 is to lump the regulatory systems representation, h_r and that of the business process, h_z. As we shall see below, this assumption has no fundamental effect on the model. Moreover, it is fairly easy to see that there is no conceptual difference between a government mandate, for example, *"These Types of Personal Information may be seen only by a Primary Care Physician"*, and an organizational business process or requirement stating that *"Payroll Data may be visible only to the Senior HR Managers"*.

Granted the business ramifications of the may be drastically different. For example, none compliance with a government mandate may invite hefty fines while a violation of business process may lead to a reprimand or even termination. These ramifications are not captured by our Systems Model, but we expect them to show up in an organization's Risk and Financial Models that we tackle in later chapters (see IAM Financial Model in Chapter 10).

Finally, our simplified generic authorization model is shown below. We have further assumed that the User is already authenticated, so that we got rid of the Authentication Model representation, h_a.

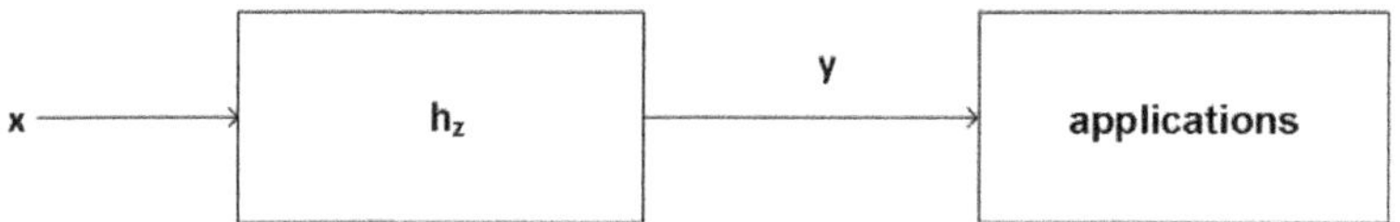

Figure 3-2: General Authorization Model Diagram

In Figure 3-2, we propose that it will be most convenient to have y represent a vector of assertions, x represent the vector of user security context, and h_z to model the conceptual combination of roles and resources.

Conceptually, we posit that:

> *The IAM System transforms the user security context into IAM assertions. The assertions are then used by applications to grant user access.*

Figure 3-2 represents the gross operation of the Authorization System, i.e. it represents a whole system operation, where "whole system" is defined here to include all users, resources and roles. Should we be concerned only about a particular user and application resource pair, all we need to do is evaluate the following symbolic function:

$$y(x_i) = h_z(..)x_i \qquad \textbf{(3-2)}$$

where we have deliberately left h_z unspecified and without any parameters or arguments until we complete our model. Nonetheless, Equation (3-2) suggests that

- ➢ h_z is or contains an operator – the operator dictates what business or regulatory driven operations need to be done on the user record, x_i, to obtain the assertions the user requires to access particular resources.
- ➢ h_z has the form of a matrix or system – in fact this is also suggested by a well-known process that organizations go through – building an access control matrix (or role mining) when implementing their Roles Based Access Management (RBAM) regime or framework.
- ➢ Comparing Equation (3-2) which shows a user authorization and Equation (2-17) which describes the results of an authentication, reproduced below, Equation (3-3):

$$y[n] = \vec{h}_a[n] * \vec{x}_i[n] \tag{3-3}$$

suggests that the User object remains invariant as it propagates through the IAM system. This observation should match everyday experience within enterprise systems; thus, regardless of how many transformations are done on the user record, the identity itself remains unchanged. Indeed Identity Management Systems or frameworks resort to using a single globally unique identifier, the Globally Unique Identifier (GUID) or Token and attach it to the user record in each store or system that the user resides in.

In the following sections, we shall derive the representation of h_z beginning with two short and very basic primers on Operator Calculus and Linear Algebra.

LINEAR OPERATOR CALCULUS PRIMER

In Mathematics or Mathematical Physics, an operator is a function that acts on another function in a consistent and well defined manner. Indeed, an operator is the same as the generalized function we first encountered in Chapter 2, under section *Modeling Authentication.*

The best way to understand operators is to use a simple example from elementary calculus. The differential operator is defined as a differentiation function:

$$\frac{d}{dx} \qquad \textbf{(3-4)}$$

Where d denotes the operator name (differential or derivative) and x is the dependent variable. Equation (3-4) is taken to mean "take the derivative of". In high school calculus, we often encountered the differential operator in the context of the function it was operating on, for example:

$$\frac{dy}{dx} \qquad \textbf{(3-5)}$$

Note that the differential operator is a separate and distinct entity from the functions it acts upon. This abstraction allows us, for example, to analyze and understand the properties of the operators themselves. We may for example come up with the following algebraic operation:

$$\left(\frac{d}{dx}+\frac{d}{dt}\right)(f(x,t)+g(x,t)) \tag{3-6}$$

In Equation (3-6), we treat operators on the left just as if they were algebraic quantities, and in fact we may expand the equation as follows:

$$\left(\frac{d}{dx}+\frac{d}{dt}\right)(f(x,t)+g(x,t)) = \frac{d}{dx}(f(x,t)+g(x,t))+\frac{d}{dt}(f(x,t)+g(x,t)) \tag{3-7}$$

which we may yet again expand as:

$$\frac{d}{dx}(f(x,t)+g(x,t))+\frac{d}{dt}(f(x,t)+g(x,t)) = \frac{df(x,t)}{dx}+\frac{dg(x,t)}{dx}+\frac{df(x,t)}{dt}+\frac{dg(x,t)}{dt} \tag{3-8}$$

whereby, we notice that each term on the right of Equation (3-8) is exactly in the familiar form, Equation (3-5).

Lastly, we note that our example operator is linear because it does not distort the *form* of the function. This is best illustrated by a simple example.

Let's imagine a linear function that takes any circle and resizes it to make it smaller. If we call this function, $R(circle)$, we can easily visualize it taking a circle and making it uniformly smaller without any distortion - Figure 3-3:

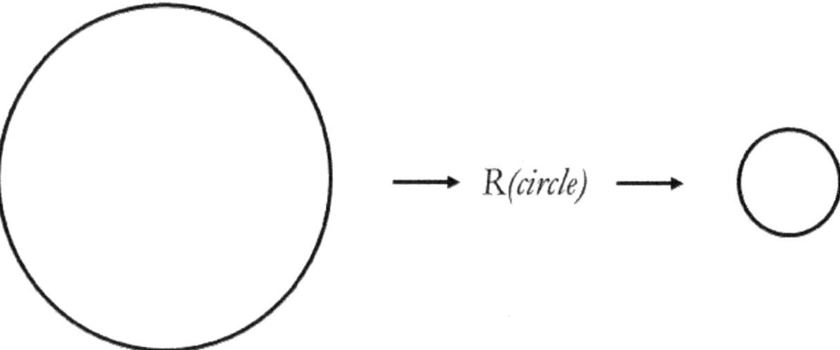

Figure 3-3: An Example of a Linear Operator.

If, for example, the function distorted the circle in the process of resizing it, the operator would not be linear - Figure 3-4:

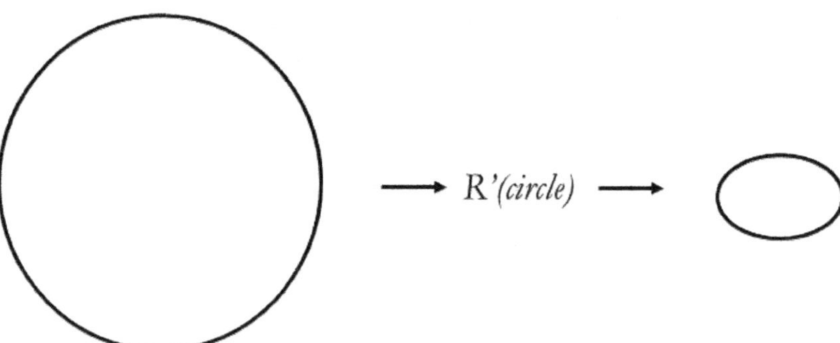

Figure 3-4: An Example of a Non-Linear Operator.

In this book, we will be dealing only with the linear operators. And that is the full extent of Operator Calculus we will need to model IAM Authorization below.

LINEAR ALGEBRA PRIMER

A common example of a word problem from high school math would go as follows:

Campus Express offers college students summer charter trips in Europe. The company flies three kinds of airplanes: the Airbus 100, the Airbus 200, and the Airbus 300. Each plane is outfitted with tourist, economy, and first-class seats.

The number of each kind of seat in the three types of planes is shown below. The second chart lists the number of reservations for its July flight to France. How many of each kind of plane should the company fly to fill all the seats?

	Airbus 100	Airbus 200	Airbus 300
Tourist	50	75	40
Economy	30	45	25
First Class	32	50	30

Category	Number of reservations
Tourist Class	305
Economy Class	185
First Class	206

As a first step towards solving this problem, we may assign the unknowns (the number of each kind of plane) the following variables:

	Airbus 100	Airbus 200	Airbus 300
Total number	x	y	z

We can then express these unknowns in terms of the known quantities in the first two tables. For example, since there are 305 reservations for the Tourist class, all we need to do to figure out how many planes of each type to fly is to simply multiply the number of planes (x, y or z) times the per-airplane number and this must the total number of Tourist Class reservations:

$$50x + 75y + 40z = 305 \quad \textbf{(3-9)}$$

Similar equations for the other cabin classes yield:

$$30x + 45y + 25z = 185 \quad \textbf{(3-10)}$$

and

$$32x + 50y + 30z = 206 \quad \textbf{(3-11)}$$

Equations (3-9) to (3-11) form a system of three equations in three unknowns, and since the number of unknowns is equal to the number of equations, a unique solution exists for x, y and z according to a fundamental theorem in mathematics, and we may arrive at the solution using elementary substitution methods.

We may also use an alternative form that treats these equations as a whole "System", as depicted below:

$$\begin{bmatrix} 50 & 75 & 40 \\ 30 & 45 & 25 \\ 32 & 50 & 30 \end{bmatrix} \begin{bmatrix} x \\ y \\ z \end{bmatrix} = \begin{bmatrix} 305 \\ 185 \\ 206 \end{bmatrix} \quad \textbf{(3-12)}$$

Equation (3-12) represents the same information as Equations (3-9) to (3-11) by relating the unknown input vector:

$$\begin{bmatrix} x \\ y \\ z \end{bmatrix} = unknown\ input\ vector \quad \textbf{(3-13)}$$

a known output vector,

$$\begin{bmatrix} 305 \\ 185 \\ 206 \end{bmatrix} = known\ output\ vector \quad \textbf{(3-14)}$$

and a *matrix* that determines the relationship between the input and output vectors:

$$\begin{bmatrix} 50 & 75 & 40 \\ 30 & 45 & 25 \\ 32 & 50 & 30 \end{bmatrix} = Relationship\ Matrix\ (The\ System) \quad \textbf{(3-15)}$$

*For our purposes, we note that Equation (3-12) is interpreted as The System in Equation (3-15) operating on the input in Equation (3-13) to produce the output of Equation (3-14). What the System "**does**" is an intrinsic property that does not depend on the input, and is completely characterized by the System Matrix in Equation (3-15).*

We may generalize the concept behind Equations (3-12) to higher dimensions as follows:

$$\begin{bmatrix} y_1 \\ \\ \cdots \\ \\ y_n \end{bmatrix} = \begin{bmatrix} h_{11} & h_{12} & \cdots & h_{1n} \\ h_{21} & h_{22} & & \cdots \\ \cdots & & & \\ & & & \\ h_{m1} & \cdots & & h_{mn} \end{bmatrix} \begin{bmatrix} x_1 \\ \\ \cdots \\ \\ x_n \end{bmatrix} \quad \textbf{(3-16)}$$

To get the output vector, we multiply and add corresponding rows and columns in the System and the input, for example:

$$y_1 = h_{11}x_1 + h_{12}x_2 + \cdots + h_{1n}x_n \quad \textbf{(3-17)}$$

Or more generally,

$$y_i = \sum_{j=1}^{j=n} h_{ij}x_j \quad \textbf{(3-18)}$$

Lastly, we note from Equation (3-12) that we can in principle invert the expression in such a way that we can immediately write down the solution through matrix multiplication.

To do this, we would proceed as follows – (the math to accomplish this would take us away from our present topic without adding much value, so we simply sketch a framework to allow the reader to understand the main concepts being conveyed here):

1. We first find another matrix of the same dimension as our System Matrix and multiply both sides of Equation (3-12) from the left (since the order of multiplication matters when dealing with matrices):

$$\begin{bmatrix} ? & ? & ? \\ ? & ? & ? \\ ? & ? & ? \end{bmatrix}\begin{bmatrix} 50 & 75 & 40 \\ 30 & 45 & 25 \\ 32 & 50 & 30 \end{bmatrix}\begin{bmatrix} x \\ y \\ z \end{bmatrix} = \begin{bmatrix} ? & ? & ? \\ ? & ? & ? \\ ? & ? & ? \end{bmatrix}\begin{bmatrix} 305 \\ 185 \\ 206 \end{bmatrix} \qquad \textbf{(3-19)}$$

2. We then arrange for the left side to be equal to the Identity Matrix (that is a matrix of all 1's along the diagonal and 0's elsewhere), by judiciously selecting the unknown matrix:

$$\begin{bmatrix} ? & ? & ? \\ ? & ? & ? \\ ? & ? & ? \end{bmatrix}\begin{bmatrix} 50 & 75 & 40 \\ 30 & 45 & 25 \\ 32 & 50 & 30 \end{bmatrix} = \begin{bmatrix} 1 & 0 & 0 \\ 0 & 1 & 0 \\ 0 & 0 & 1 \end{bmatrix} \qquad \textbf{(3-20)}$$

3. Equation (3-19) then becomes (via substitution from Equation (3-20))

$$\begin{bmatrix} 1 & 0 & 0 \\ 0 & 1 & 0 \\ 0 & 0 & 1 \end{bmatrix}\begin{bmatrix} x \\ y \\ z \end{bmatrix} = \begin{bmatrix} ? & ? & ? \\ ? & ? & ? \\ ? & ? & ? \end{bmatrix}\begin{bmatrix} 305 \\ 185 \\ 206 \end{bmatrix} \qquad \textbf{(3-21)}$$

4. Equation (3-21) simplifies, after the left hand multiplication, which in the matrix world is like multiplication by 1 in the regular number multiplication terms, to

$$\begin{bmatrix} x \\ y \\ z \end{bmatrix} = \begin{bmatrix} ? & ? & ? \\ ? & ? & ? \\ ? & ? & ? \end{bmatrix} \begin{bmatrix} 305 \\ 185 \\ 206 \end{bmatrix} \tag{3-22}$$

We interpret equation (3-22) as generating a new System Matrix that transforms the output to yield back the input.

We may also think of Equation (3-22) as a reverse engineering of the original System. We depict these two operations below visually, which applies for any input $\begin{bmatrix} x \\ y \\ z \end{bmatrix}$, and where we have solved for the unknown matrix:

$$\begin{bmatrix} ? & ? & ? \\ ? & ? & ? \\ ? & ? & ? \end{bmatrix} = \begin{bmatrix} -1.0 & 2.5 & -0.75 \\ 1.0 & 2.2 & 0.5 \\ -0.6 & 1.0 & 0.0 \end{bmatrix} \tag{3-23}$$

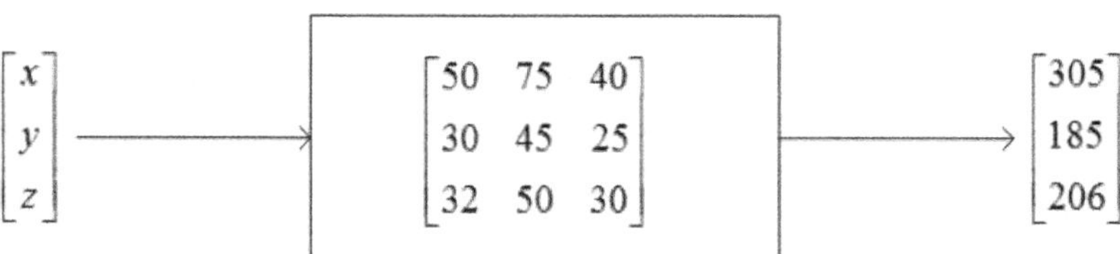

Figure 3-5: Linear Systems Matrix Representation of a Linear System of Equations.

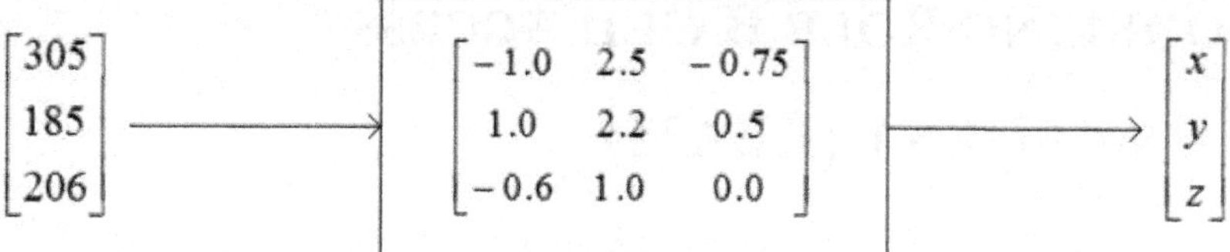

Figure 3-6: Linear Systems Matrix Representation (Inverted or run backwards)

The process of reversing a system involves what is termed as calculating the *Outer Product* of two vectors, which as you will see below, results in a Matrix (or System in our model):

Formally, the outer product of two vectors $\vec{u}$ and $\vec{v}$ is defined as (using a 3-dimensional example):

$$\vec{u}\vec{v} = \begin{bmatrix} u_1 \\ u_2 \\ u_3 \end{bmatrix} \begin{bmatrix} v_1 & v_2 & v_3 \end{bmatrix} = \begin{bmatrix} u_1v_1 & u_1v_2 & u_1v_3 \\ u_2v_1 & u_2v_2 & u_2v_3 \\ u_3v_1 & u_3v_2 & u_3v_3 \end{bmatrix} \quad \textbf{(3-24)}$$

Or more generally,

$$\vec{u}\vec{v} = \begin{bmatrix} u_1 \\ \cdots \\ u_m \end{bmatrix} \begin{bmatrix} v_1 & \cdots & v_n \end{bmatrix} = \begin{bmatrix} u_1v_1 & \cdots & u_1v_n \\ \cdots & u_iv_j & \cdots \\ u_mv_1 & \cdots & u_mv_n \end{bmatrix} \quad \textbf{(3-25)}$$

MODELING ROLE BASED ACCESS MANAGEMENT (RBAM)

In RBAM, roles are created that mirror business requirements, policies, standards and regulatory mandates. Such roles are then assigned or mapped to resources, while users are added or removed from the roles based on the their organizational responsibilities.

From a conceptual point of view, a Role may be defined rather abstractly – see the sources already cited, (Ferraiolo, D., Barkely, J., & Kuhn, D, 1999), (Nyanchama, M, & Osborn, S, 1999), and (Zhang, Z., Zhang, X., Sandhu, R., 2007). However, the roles must eventually be actualized or computed in some way for the IAM System to do something useful with them. There are several ways to accomplish this and we start by giving a few examples to make our model concrete:

- The "Manager" Role may be defined as LDAP users who have the *employeeType* attribute set to some string, say, "Manager". The manner in which the role is actualized depends on implementation and scenario. The IAM System may, for example, perform an LDAP search, *(employeeType=Manager)* and return all users who fit the role, or if the IAM System has a user context already, it may just search LDAP for that one user and the attribute, for example *(&(employeeType=Manager)(uid=123456789))*.

- The Role "Financial Approver" may involve a complex calculation and sophisticated business modeling that rely on real time as well as historical organizational and industry data to determine some metric threshold that the holder of the role must meet in order to be assigned the role that approves or otherwise financially obligates the firm and at what level/amount.

- A Role called "Password Manager" may stipulate that the User should only have access to application screens that allow the holder to reset a user's password. All other Personal Information, including the user's password, will be hidden from the holder of this role. Such a role may stem, say, from a government rule mandating that personal information of passport applications be hidden from everyone, including IT staff.

- The Role "Check Writer" may contain conditions on the holder stating that they may not also hold the "Check Approver" role. This may result, for example, from financial separation of duties (SoD) controls that the organization has put in place to avoid financial fraud, and that are enforced by the IAM System.

As we can see in these examples, the actual definition of a role may be quite broad in order to allow for arbitrary business requirements, standards and policies to be defined precisely and implemented accordingly. The evolution of the roles may also involve an elaborate process of interpreting the organization structure, business requirements and government regulations that govern the industry.

Once evolved and designed, the purely conceptual roles are mapped to the organization resources. The basic framework is to state, via an organizational policy, which roles are allowed to access which resources. From an implementation perspective, the IAM System would then build a policy database that contains all the roles and the resources they apply to. Such a database is consulted before a user is allowed access to a resource.

Modeling Organizational Roles

To start conceptualizing and organizing our model, we will represent all the organization's roles in a vector as follows:

$$\vec{T} = \begin{bmatrix} t_1 \\ \\ \cdots \\ \\ t_m \end{bmatrix} \qquad \textbf{(3-26)}$$

If we now recall that roles actually represent actions, it is easy to see that Equation (3-26) is actually a vector of *operators*, each element of which represents a distinct role in the organization.

The clearest way to convince ourselves that Equation (3-26) is a vector of operators is to examine the examples of the roles given above, all which call for some action to be performed on the resources (and eventually, the user). This is the very definition of an operator from *Linear Operator Calculus* section above.

Modeling Organizational Resources

Resources may be defined broadly to mean any information or system that the user may desire access to. IAM Systems normally work with resources that may be expressed as strings (say Uniform Resource Identifiers or URIs), but a resource may also be an element or even an elemental value within a document (page).

Regardless of how fine grained the definition of a resource is, the conceptual treatment is fairly simple: a static vector that we shall call $\vec{R}$.

$$\vec{R} = \begin{bmatrix} r_1 \\ \\ \cdots \\ \\ r_n \end{bmatrix} \quad \textbf{(3-27)}$$

THE IAM SYSTEM AUTHORIZATION MODEL

By prior arguments, we know from Equation (3-2) that the IAM System Authorization Model must have the form

$$y(x_i) = h_z(\dots)x_i \qquad \textbf{(3-28)}$$

Given the discussion in the last two sections, we may conjecture that $h_z(\dots)$ must contain the Roles and Resource information. It must also be a System since we know from practice that IAM authorizations involve operations on the user and resources she seeks to access.

Given these suppositions, which remain to be proven at this point, we have only one possible form or expression for $h_z(\dots)$:

$h_z(\dots)$ must be the outer product of the Roles Operator and the Resource vectors, according to Equation (3-25):

$$\vec{u}\vec{v} = \begin{bmatrix} u_1 \\ \dots \\ u_m \end{bmatrix} [v_1 \quad \dots \quad v_n] = \begin{bmatrix} u_1 v_1 & \dots & u_1 v_n \\ \dots & u_i v_j & \dots \\ u_m v_1 & \dots & u_m v_n \end{bmatrix} \qquad \textbf{(3-29)}$$

i.e.

$$h_z(\dots) = \vec{T}\vec{R} \qquad \textbf{(3-30)}$$

or

$$h_z(\ldots) = \begin{bmatrix} t_1 \\ \\ \cdots \\ \\ t_m \end{bmatrix} [r_1 \quad \cdots \quad r_n] = \begin{bmatrix} t_1r_1 & t_1r_2 & \cdots & t_1r_n \\ t_2r_1 & t_2r_2 & \cdots & \cdots \\ \cdots & \cdots & \cdots & \\ & & t_ir_j & \cdots \\ t_mr_1 & t_mr_1 & \cdots & t_mr_n \end{bmatrix} \quad \textbf{(3-31)}$$

Equation (3-31) is the ***Authorization System Matrix***. It dictates what operators need to be applied to each resource to allow access to them.

Note:

We have not strictly derived or proven the Authorization System Matrix, Equation (3-31), in a rigorous manner. Rather, we have deduced that it must have that form based on our assumptions. This is valid for our purposes, namely that it matches the operation of a real IAM system, and may be considered as a form of deductive reasoning and/or proof.

§§

To complete the model, we need to incorporate the user information. We determine the form it takes below.

For illustration purposes, we reduce Equation (3-31) to the following simpler 2x2 System before generalizing:

$$h_z(..) = \begin{bmatrix} t_1 \\ t_2 \end{bmatrix} \begin{bmatrix} r_1 & r_2 \end{bmatrix} = \begin{bmatrix} t_1 r_1 & t_1 r_2 \\ t_2 r_1 & t_2 r_2 \end{bmatrix} \qquad \textbf{(3-32)}$$

i.e. our simplified IAM Authorization System has only two roles and two resources.

We notice the following:

- From a practical perspective, we know that the Operators above have to be applied to some attribute or property of the user, such that user information must be incorporated into Equation (3-32) according to Equation (3-2) to get the complete model.

- Since there are two roles and two resources, we expect there to be at most $m * n$ *or* $2 * 2 = 4$ assertions. Each role may potentially apply to each resource, and thus there are a total of $2 * 2$ combinations of roles and resources possible.

- If the user x_i accessed both resources, the System would in theory have to calculate all the four assertions:

$$y_{11} = t_1 r_1 x_i \tag{3-33}$$

$$y_{12} = t_1 r_2 x_i \tag{3-34}$$

$$y_{21} = t_2 r_1 x_i \tag{3-35}$$

$$y_{22} = t_2 r_2 x_i \tag{3-36}$$

- The above equations suggest that the gross System interaction may be described as follows:

$$\begin{bmatrix} y_{11} & y_{12} \\ y_{21} & y_{22} \end{bmatrix} = \begin{bmatrix} t_1 r_1 & t_1 r_2 \\ t_2 r_1 & t_2 r_2 \end{bmatrix} \begin{bmatrix} x_i & 0 \\ 0 & x_i \end{bmatrix} \tag{3-37}$$

- We may write the last term in Equation (3-37) as:

$$\begin{bmatrix} x_i & 0 \\ 0 & x_i \end{bmatrix} = \begin{bmatrix} 1 & 0 \\ 0 & 1 \end{bmatrix} x_i \tag{3-38}$$

where we have used the Identity Matrix of size 2.

Equations (3-37) and (3-38) suggest that for any given user x_i, and an IAM System that consists of t_m roles and r_n resources, his interaction with the IAM Authorization System should be expressed as follows:

$$\begin{bmatrix} y_{11} & y_{12} & \dots & y_{1n} \\ y_{21} & y_{22} & \dots & \dots \\ \dots & \dots & \dots & \\ & & y_{ij} & \dots \\ y_{m1} & y_{m2} & \dots & y_{mn} \end{bmatrix} = \begin{bmatrix} t_1r_1 & t_1r_2 & \dots & t_1r_n \\ t_2r_1 & t_2r_2 & \dots & \dots \\ \dots & \dots & \dots & \\ & & t_ir_j & \dots \\ t_mr_1 & t_mr_1 & \dots & t_mr_n \end{bmatrix} \begin{bmatrix} 1 & 0 & \dots & 0 \\ 0 & 1 & \dots & \dots \\ \dots & \dots & \dots & \\ & & 1 & \dots \\ 0 & 0 & \dots & 1 \end{bmatrix} x_i \quad \textbf{(3-39)}$$

In Equation (3-39), the last matrix is the $n * n$ Identity matrix, often represented as $\boldsymbol{I_n}$.

Equation (3-39) completes our conceptual authorization model. In the next section, we attempt to understand what it means in some detail.

IAM AUTHORIZATION SYSTEM INTERPRETATION

Equation (3-39) represents the entire interaction between a user x_i and the IAM Authorization System that that has a total of t_m roles and r_n resources. We may make the following qualitative statements about the structure and nature of the RBAM authorization system.

Each term in the output matrix on the left represents an assertion produced by applying the correspondingly ordered role on the user and corresponding resource. For example,

$$y_{ij} = t_i(r_j x_i) \tag{3-40}$$

which may be interpreted as an assertion for the user x_i with regards to the resource r_j based on the role t_i.

We have written (3-40) to emphasize the fact that the role operator is applied to the user and resource combination. Nonetheless, one may wonder what Equation (3-40) means in practice. To make progress on that, we need to expand it and completely evaluate it. If such an expansion turns out to be consistent with the physical process of authorizing a user to a resource based on a role in a real world IAM System, then we can have some confidence that our model is based on a solid foundation.

We sketch a simple approach below, noting that perhaps more

sophisticated examples may be derived from the same conceptual foundation outlined above:

- An access policy is defined on resources using a role as the basis (or a role is mapped to a resource)
- A role is assigned to a user.
- When a user tries to access a resource, the IAM System checks to see if they hold a role that matches the role or set or roles that are permitted for the resource.

One way to ***define*** an assertion that meets these requirements would be as follows:

$$y_{11} = t_1(r_1 x_i) \equiv t_1 x_i + t_1 r_1 \qquad \textbf{(3-41)}$$

Note that Equation (3-41) may be fully evaluated as follows, bearing in mind that t_1 is a role operator:

$$t_1 x_i = \begin{cases} 0.5 \; if\ role\ is\ assigned\ to\ user \\ 0.0 \; if\ role\ is\ not\ assigned\ to\ user \end{cases} \qquad \textbf{(3-42)}$$

$$t_1 r_1 = \begin{cases} 0.5 \; if\ role\ is\ mapped\ to\ resource \\ 0.0 \; if\ role\ is\ not\ mapped\ to\ resource \end{cases} \qquad \textbf{(3-43)}$$

In Equation (3-42) and Equation (3-43), we have chosen an arbitrary quantization level of 0.5 for later convenience.

Substituting Equations (3-42) and Equation (3-43) into Equation (3-41), we get simply:

$$y_{11} = \begin{cases} 1.0 \; user\ has\ role\ and\ role\ is\ mapped\ to\ resource \\ 0.5 \; user\ has\ role\ but\ role\ is\ not\ mapped\ to\ resource \\ 0.5 \; user\ does\ not\ have\ role, role\ is\ mapped\ to\ resource \\ 0.0 \; otherwise \end{cases} \quad \textbf{(3-44)}$$

We may further quantize/digitize these quaternaries (using the 0.75 quantum) since we are only interested in the scenario whereby the user has the role *and* the role is mapped to the resource vis a vis all other scenarios, a process that is essentially binary.

This quantization approach results in:

$$y_{11} = \begin{cases} 1.0 \; user\ has\ role\ and\ role\ is\ mapped\ to\ resource \\ 0.0 \; user\ has\ role\ but\ role\ is\ not\ mapped\ to\ resource \\ 0.0 \; user\ does\ not\ have\ role, role\ is\ mapped\ to\ resource \\ 0.0 \; otherwise \end{cases} \quad \textbf{(3-45)}$$

We may further convert Equation (3-46) to a binary format by discarding the two middle quanta, resulting into a simple binary result that is easily implemented:

$$y_{11} = \begin{cases} 1.0 \; if\ the\ user\ is\ authorized \\ 0.0 \; otherwise \end{cases} \quad \textbf{(3-46)}$$

An Alternative Formulation

It is important to read Equation (3-41) as our **definition** of the roles operator t_1 operating on the combined resource and user quantity, $r_1 x_i$. Our definition will be valid as long as it corresponds to a real world IAM System. Furthermore, as we mentioned earlier, the reader should avoid interpreting Equation (3-41) in purely algebraic terms.

Nonetheless, we may alternatively proceed from Equation (3-40) as follows, akin to the differential operator:

$$y_{11} = t_1(r_1 x_i) = r_1 t_1 x_i + x_i t_1 r_1 \tag{3-47}$$

Using the results of Equations (3-42) and (3-43), Equation (3-47) may be evaluated to

$$y_{11} = \begin{cases} 0.5r_1 + 0.5x_i & \{user \rightarrow role\}, \{role \rightarrow resource\} \\ 0.5r_1 & \{user \rightarrow role\}, \{role\,!\,resource\} \\ 0.5x_i & \{user\,!\,role\}, \{role \rightarrow resource\} \\ 0 & otherwise \end{cases} \tag{3-48}$$

In Equation (3-48), we have used the shorthand $\{user \rightarrow role\}$ to denote that the role is assigned to the user, $\{role \rightarrow resource\}$ to denote the role is mapped to the resource, $\{user\,!\,role\}$ to denote that the role is not assigned to the user, and $\{role\,!\,resource\}$ to denote that the role is not mapped to the resource.

Compared to our earlier binary result which we were able to evaluate readily - Equations (3-45) and (3-46) - the difficulty of interpretation obviously lies in attaching an analytical meaning to terms $r_1 + x_i$, r_1 and x_i in Equation (3-48). But this turns out to be a simple task conceptually because we can easily evaluate them just as well.

One way to accomplish the evaluation is to perform the following symbolic division, keeping in mind that prior to authorization, the IAM System already has user identity in context, say x_i from the Authentication System h_a (Figure 3-1). Of course the resource, say r_1, would have been obtained from the request context as well. The IAM System also obtains the same information, say x_l and r_l from the organizational Policy Store for matching purposes as shown in Figure 3-7 below:

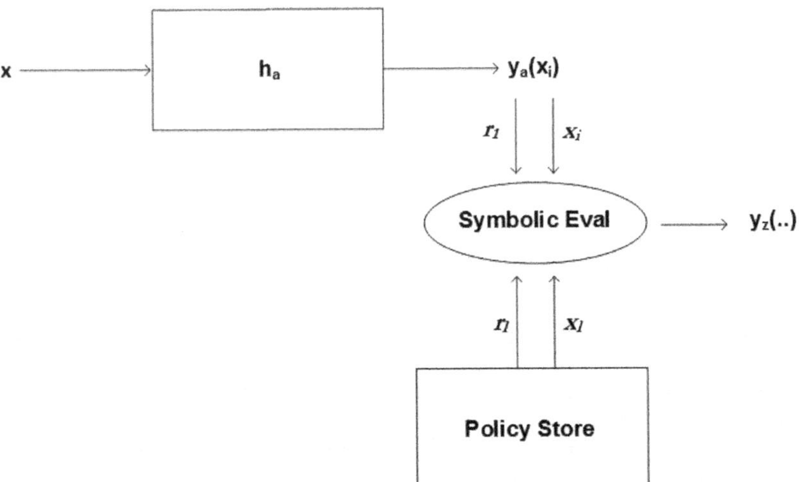

Figure 3-7: Symbolic Evaluation of Authorization Using User Context Information, $\{x_i, r_1\}$ and Stored / Reference User and Resource Data, $\{x_l, r_l\}$.

With Figure 3-7 in mind, the symbolic evaluation becomes:

$$y_{11} = \begin{cases} 0.5\dfrac{r_1}{r_l} + 0.5\dfrac{x_i}{x_l} & \{user \rightarrow role\}, \{role \rightarrow resource\} \\ 0.5\dfrac{r_1}{r_l} & \{user \rightarrow role\}, \{role \; ! \; resource\} \\ 0.5\dfrac{x_i}{x_l} & \{user \; ! \; role\}, \{role \rightarrow resource\} \\ 0 & otherwise \end{cases} \qquad \textbf{(3-49)}$$

It should then be obvious that for the properly authorized user, Equation (3-49) reduces to our prior, less rigorous result, Equation (3-45) because the following conditions will only be met if the authenticated user x_i is authorized for the resource r_1 that she requested, based on prior established organizational policies, i.e.:

$$r_1 = r_l \qquad \textbf{(3-50)}$$

$$x_i = x_l \qquad \textbf{(3-51)}$$

IN PRACTICE

Qualitative Properties of Authorization System Matrix

The main result from the last section

$$\begin{bmatrix} y_{11} & y_{12} & \dots & y_{1n} \\ y_{21} & y_{22} & \dots & \dots \\ \dots & \dots & \dots & \\ & & y_{ij} & \dots \\ y_{m1} & y_{m2} & \dots & y_{mn} \end{bmatrix} = \begin{bmatrix} t_1r_1 & t_1r_2 & \dots & t_1r_n \\ t_2r_1 & t_2r_2 & \dots & \dots \\ \dots & \dots & \dots & \\ & & t_ir_j & \dots \\ t_mr_1 & t_mr_1 & \dots & t_mr_n \end{bmatrix} \begin{bmatrix} 1 & 0 & \dots & 0 \\ 0 & 1 & \dots & \dots \\ \dots & \dots & \dots & \\ & & 1 & \dots \\ 0 & 0 & \dots & 1 \end{bmatrix} x_i \qquad \textbf{(3-52)}$$

is potentially very large matrix. It is as wide as the number of resource definitions in the IAM System, which, while the number may not be as big as the total number of actual resources (since the resource definitions are almost always generalized), is still likely to be quite large.

There are, however, several simplifying devices that we may employ to lessen any computational load associated with getting a user's assertions, since, typically, the IAM System needs to compute the user's assertions within a fairly short login window, i.e., a duration on the order of a few seconds.

The first realization to make about Equation (3-52) is that, for any particular user, the Authorization System Matrix is very sparse. In fact if we look at the Matrix, Equation (3-31), we notice that all terms except those that contain the user's roles vanish. The role operator will be zero in all those instances since the operator represents a role that the user does not have. In fact, if the roles are properly designed, any one user will have just a handful of enterprise roles (since no human being can or should be performing more than a handful of roles within the organization). At the very least, the number of roles assigned to the average user will be much smaller than the number of resource definitions.

$$Authorization\ System\ Matrix = \begin{bmatrix} t_1 r_1 & t_1 r_2 & \cdots & t_1 r_n \\ t_2 r_1 & t_2 r_2 & \cdots & \cdots \\ \cdots & \cdots & \cdots & \\ & & t_i r_j & \cdots \\ t_m r_1 & t_m r_1 & \cdots & t_m r_n \end{bmatrix} \quad \textbf{(3-53)}$$

We thus end us with an exceedingly sparse matrix, and we may apply several methods and algorithms that have been developed for sparse matrices to compute and store the user's assertions efficiently. We shall not delve further into these techniques since it would take us far from our topic, except to point out to the reader that our model is computationally practical.

The second important property of Authorization System Matrix, Equation (3-53), is that the IAM System may further reduce the size of the matrix since the user will not need to access all resources they have assertions to, at least not during the precious few seconds during and after they authenticate. This results in a further 'sparsing' of the Authorization System Matrix, and suggests a mechanism of calculating the user's assertion without impacting the user's login experience adversely.

IAM Authorization Example

Let's provide an example of how an assertion may look like in a real world implementation. Earlier, we provided the following role example:

> *The Role "Check Writer" may contain conditions on the holder stating that they may not also hold the "Check Approver" role. This may result, for example, from financial controls that the organization has put in place to avoid financial fraud, and that are enforced by the IAM System.*

From this, we need to evaluate Equation (3-41)

$$y_{11} = t_1(r_1 x_i) \equiv t_1 x_i + t_1 r_1 \qquad \textbf{(3-54)}$$

or Equation (3-47)

$$y_{11} = t_1(r_1 x_i) = r_1 t_1 x_i + x_i t_1 r_1 \qquad \textbf{(3-55)}$$

As we have shown above that they yield the same result at the end, we will use the simpler Equation (3-41).

Assume the User x_i has the following attributes:

```
# User entry x_i
dn:
uid=123456789,ou=People,ou=corp,dc=acclaimconsult
ing,dc=com
objectClass: inetOrgPerson
cn: Joe Sample
sn: Sample
mail: joe.sample@acclaimconsulting.com
employeeRole: Manager
employeeRole: HR Manager
employeeRole: Check Approver
...
```

Note that we have used the LDAP namespace (user directory), so our definition of the user is based on the identifier $uid = 123456789$:

$$
\begin{aligned}
x_i = ldap://ldap.acclaimconsulting.com{:}489/ou \\
= people, ou = corp, dc \\
= acclaimconsulting, dc = com?\,(uid \\
= 123456789)
\end{aligned}
\qquad \textbf{(3-56)}
$$

In Equation (3-56), the user context from which we build the search string ($uid = 123456789$) is assumed to be derived from the upstream authentication process, and that the namespace context $ldap://ldap.acclaimconsulting.com{:}489$ (service details – protocol, server name and port) are derived from IAM System's environmental context).

We may then proceed to define the operator needed to meet this business requirement as follows:

$$t_1 = (\&(employeeRole = Check\ Writer)!\,(employeeRole = Check\ Approver)) \quad \textbf{(3-57)}$$

Equation (3-57) is an LDAP search operation that corresponds to the stated business requirement, i.e. it restricts the role to Check Writers who are not Check Approvers.

The resource may be a Uniform Resource Locator (URL), for example, a Human Resources Check Writing Application (expressed generally, omitting environmental context):

$$r_1 = "/hr/check/" \quad \textbf{(3-58)}$$

Lastly, RBAM maps the Check Writer Role to the resource and stores this information to organization policy store. We may represent this symbolically as:

$$Check\ Writer = "/hr/check/" \quad \textbf{(3-59)}$$

Finally and simply:

$$t_1x_i = ldap://ldap.acclaimconsulting.com:489/ou = people, ou = corp, dc = acclaimconsulting, dc = com?(uid = 123456789)(\&(employeeRole = Check\ Writer)!(employeeRole = Check\ Approver)) \tag{3-60}$$

and

$$t_1r_1 = (\&(employeeRole = Check\ Writer)!(employeeRole = Check\ Approver))(Check\ Writer = "/hr/check/") \tag{3-61}$$

Equation (3-60) will return a non-zero (non-null) entry only if the user has the *Check Writer* Role and does not have the *Check Approver* Role. In LDAP it returns the user record in the first instance, and zero in all other cases.

Even though Equation (3-61) must be interpreted symbolically to make any sense of it, there is no conceptual difficulty - it will yield a non-zero result only if the role is mapped to the resource.

SUMMARY

In this chapter we analyzed user authorization in a generalized IAM System. Our main result in this chapter derived an IAM System Authorization Matrix, a property of the system that determines who is authorized to what resources, and that may be derived from the outer product of the roles operator and the resource vector.

Chapter 4 – Modeling IAM Controls: Access Reviews and Certification

INTRODUCTION

Up to this point, we have modeled the so called *enforcement control* functions of an IAM System, namely Authentication and Authorization. These two important functions provide crucial checkpoints within the enterprise, ensuring that only those properly authenticated to the enterprise and authorized to a specific application or resource are allowed in.

The user assertions of Chapter 3, Equation (3-39) (the user's roles+resources) are typically assigned during the on-boarding process. However, in the lifecycle of an identity, the user's roles and responsibilities change such that the initial roles become invalid, redundant or outright dangerous. The processes of Access Reviews and Certification provide a means to periodically evaluate the current user entitlements and access to make sure that they are in-line with the user's current role (See for example, Osmanoglu 2014). Together with Data Governance, these functions form the *detective controls and preventive controls* aspect of IAM, in a sense providing a third party, out-of-band check to ensure that there is verifiable consistency between the organization's documented requirements, standards and policies on the one hand, and their implementation in terms of IAM Systems architecture, design and implementation.

A good example of evolving roles is to suppose that the employee Jessica is hired as a Systems Administrator. She is assigned the System Administrator Role that gives her access to all Active Directory Domains and root access to all Linux Web Servers. Two years later, she gets promoted to IT Manager and a new Systems Administrator Joe is hired to take over her former role. Unless an Access Review and Certification is done to remove System Administrator Role from Jessica, the organization runs a risk *ipso facto* because an employee now has more roles than they need to do their work, assuming the IT Manager has no Systems Administrator responsibility, and thereby violating the principle that a user should only be given the minimum level of access for them to perform their duties.

It is important to note that detective controls and preventive controls are not so much about correcting inherent problems within the organization's role engineering processes; rather, as the names suggest, Access Review and Certification is about providing a "third party", out of band way to verify that the right roles are assigned to the right users and mapped to the right resources. It is a way to minimize risk, especially in financial departments or IT where a user with the wrong role or a toxic combination of roles may cause tremendous damage to the organization.

A natural question may arise as to which system will police our detective controls and preventive controls systems? Well the answer is that in practice, one level of policing via detective/preventive controls is normally sufficient for most purposes and organizations. However, depending on system or data risk and sensitivity, multiple ringed layers of controls may be implemented.

We depict these concepts below, Figure 4-1. In the figure, $A(x,t)$ is the Authorization Roles Matrix from Equation (3-39), Chapter 3, reproduced below, and $A'(x,t)$ is the matrix after detective/preventive controls process has removed un-needed roles, toxic combination of roles or some such roles that should not be assigned to this user, per organization's requirements, standards and policies.

$$A(x_i,t) = \begin{bmatrix} t_1r_1 & t_1r_2 & \dots & t_1r_n \\ t_2r_1 & t_2r_2 & \dots & \dots \\ \dots & \dots & \dots & \\ & & t_ir_j & \dots \\ t_mr_1 & t_mr_1 & \dots & t_mr_n \end{bmatrix} \begin{bmatrix} 1 & 0 & \dots & 0 \\ 0 & 1 & \dots & \dots \\ \dots & \dots & \dots & \\ & & 1 & \dots \\ 0 & 0 & \dots & 1 \end{bmatrix} x_i \qquad \textbf{(4-1)}$$

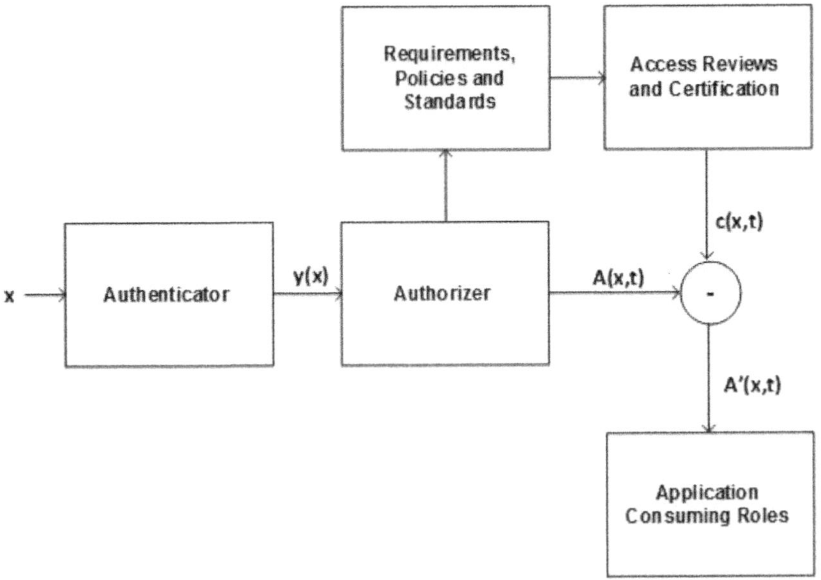

Figure 4-1: Detective and Preventive Controls System, For Example, Interrogating the User Roles and Removing Inappropriate Roles or Toxic Combinations.

As before, our primary question is whether we can apply systems engineering principles to model detective controls and preventive controls rather than an exhaustive treatise on current trends in Access Reviews and Certification practice.

A Modeling of IAM Controls

Perhaps a place to start our detective model is Figure 4-1 where a cursory examination might reveal that if $c(x,t)$ is the detective or preventive control that, in our example, removes unneeded roles or toxic role combination from the user's Authorization Roles Matrix, then the corrected matrix, $A'(x,t)$, must be given by:

$$A'(x,t) = A(x,t) - c(x,t) \tag{4-2}$$

As simple as Equation (4-2) is, we can immediately model several classes of IAM detective and preventive controls. These include

- Detective and preventive controls that prohibit a specific combination of roles because doing so may bypass organizational check and balances or some such accountability policies. The classic example involves a user who is both a check writer and a check approver.

Assume for example that

$$t_1 = Check\ Writer \tag{4-3}$$

$$t_2 = Check\ Approver \tag{4-4}$$

then if we recall from Equation (3-26), Chapter 3, that the roles are given by

$$\vec{T} = \begin{bmatrix} t_1 \\ t_2 \\ \dots \\ \\ t_m \end{bmatrix} \tag{4-5}$$

it is easy to see that selecting the detective and preventive control roles matrix, $\vec{C}$, as follows

$$\vec{C} = \begin{bmatrix} t_1 \\ t_2 \\ \dots \\ 0 \\ 0 \end{bmatrix} \tag{4-6}$$

leads to, following Equation (3-31), Chapter 3,

$$h_z(\dots) = \begin{bmatrix} t_1 - t_1 \\ t_2 - t_2 \\ \dots \\ \\ t_m \end{bmatrix} [r_1 \quad \dots \quad r_n] = \begin{bmatrix} 0 & 0 & \dots & 0 \\ 0 & 0 & \dots & 0 \\ t_3 r_1 & t_3 r_2 & \dots & t_3 r_n \\ \dots & \dots & t_i r_j & \dots \\ t_m r_1 & t_m r_1 & \dots & t_m r_n \end{bmatrix} \tag{4-7}$$

and finally

$$A'(x,t) = \begin{bmatrix} 0 & 0 & \dots & 0 \\ 0 & 0 & \dots & 0 \\ t_3 r_1 & t_3 r_2 & \dots & t_3 r_n \\ \dots & \dots & t_i r_j & \dots \\ t_m r_1 & t_m r_1 & \dots & t_m r_n \end{bmatrix} \begin{bmatrix} 1 & 0 & \dots & 0 \\ 0 & 1 & \dots & \dots \\ \dots & \dots & \dots & \\ & & 1 & \dots \\ 0 & 0 & \dots & 1 \end{bmatrix} x_i \tag{4-8}$$

From which Equation (4-8), it is rather obvious that the user's previously assigned toxic combination of roles, $\{t_1, t_2\}$ has been removed.

- Using similar basic modeling, it is possible to impose an arbitrary set of controls to suit virtually any controls regime.

  - For example, we can specify that no one in the Accounting Department, role $t_a = \mathit{Accounting}$, may also be an IT Systems Administrator, role $t_b = \mathit{Systems\ Administrator}$, if they are in management, role $t_c = \mathit{Manager}$.

- It is also possible to *add* a role to a user's Authorization Roles Matrix using our model. This may be useful, for example, as a detective control for the so-called birthright roles - the IAM System roles that every user in a department or organization is assigned simply by virtue of belonging. Typically these roles are assigned during the onboarding process, nonetheless, a detective control may be used to add the role if it is detected that a user does not have a birthright role for whatever reason.

  A detective role of this type may also be used as part of a complex detective control. In the example above, Equation (4-8), an organization may decide that if the toxic combination $\{t_1 = \mathit{Check\ Writer}, t_2 = \mathit{Check\ Approver}\}$ is found during an Access Review campaign, the detective control should remove just the more toxic role of the pair, namely the *Check Approver* role, such that the overall organization risk is lowered.

Note:

In the example leading to Equation (4-8), we have removed the toxic combination $\{t_1, t_2\}$. *But we have also removed access to all resources that either role was mapped to. This may be undesirable, for example, if the same role is mapped to multiple applications and it role combination toxicity depends on the application. We will address this below.*

Modeling Automated IAM Controls

The previous model of IAM Controls works for the most part, but a careful examination will quickly reveal that unless we know exactly what corrective controls to apply and when to invoke them, our detective and preventive system is bound to fail or at least lag behind our control objective. In other words, the control mechanism is systemically manual in the sense that the control mechanism of Figure 4-1 requires that we prepare the detective and preventive control roles matrix of Equation (4-6). Even more critically, we have created a loophole whereby $A(x,t)$ may not be corrected in a timely manner because $c(x,t)$ arrived too late! The classic example of this phenomenon is a law abiding driver on a highway intent on maintaining the speed limit of 60 mph by manually throttling the speed pedal: regardless of what he does, he will find himself either traveling below the speed limit or above it for the most part.

What he really needs is cruise control!

The Reference Authorization Roles Matrix

The first concept we need to capture is the Reference Authorization Roles Matrix, $R(x_i, t)$. For any user and set of resources, $R(x_i, t)$ is our understanding of the true entitlement of the user given the current $(time = t)$ organizational requirements, standards, policies and the user's job function. The Reference Authorization Roles Matrix is different and distinct from the Authorization Roles Matrix of Equation (4-1) because they are the results of two distinct organizational processes.

Reference Authorization Roles Matrix, is what the user's Authorization Roles Matrix *should be.* It is the product of the organization implementing detective and preventive controls to ensure that the organization as a whole is living up to its standards and policies. As an example, an automated Segregation of Duties (SoD) IAM sub-system may be implemented that, based on written policies defined in Risk Department working with an external auditor, spell out a set of rules that must be followed while assigning roles to users. The SoD sub-system, as a detective and preventive control, may then be applied post Role Engineering to ensure that its mandates are always met. Another example may be a quarterly Access Review whereby each Manager is required to Certify that her direct reports' assigned roles are continuously relevant to their current job function.

The Actual Authorization Roles Matrix

The Actual Authorization Roles Matrix, on the other hand, what is the user's Authorization Roles Matrix *is*. It is the product of Role Engineering as we have previously discussed, and captured in Equation (4-1). During the process of onboarding, job transfer or job termination, the IAM System automatically assigns the user the appropriate Authorization Roles Matrix for their new job function. Role Engineering may involve, for example, running a tool that crawls through the corporate LDAP directory and every time it finds a manager, $title = Manager$ in a particular cost center, say $costCenter = 98765$, an enterprise role called $Role = 98765\ Approver$ is automatically created and added to the Enterprise Roles Catalog. The role may then be used in a financial application in an expense approval workflow for employees in that cost center.

We depict these ideas below, Figure 4-2, where

$A(x_i, t)$ is the Actual Authorization Roles Matrix,

$R(x_i, t)$ is the Reference Authorization Roles Matrix, and

$E(x_i, t)$ is the difference between $R(x_i, t)$ and $A(x_i, t)$, i.e. the error between what was designed and what it should be.

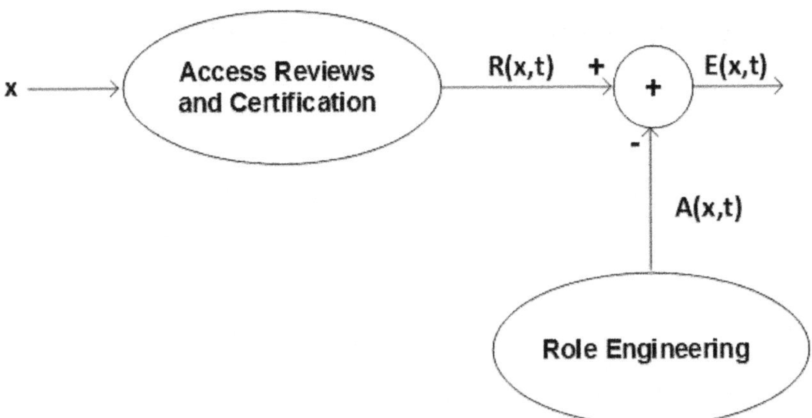

Figure 4-2: Relationship Between Actual Authorization Roles Matrix and the Reference Authorization Roles Matrix.

Completing The Model: Control Objective

From Figure 4-2, it should be obvious that the control objective, just like that of a car's cruise control, is to make sure that the Actual Authorization Roles Matrix is as close as possible to the Reference Authorization Roles Matrix. In other equation form,

Control Objective:

$$A(x,t) \approx R(x,t) \qquad \textbf{(4-9)}$$

Equation (4-9) is the best we can do from a Systems Engineering perspective: we can drive the error as small as possible, see below, but we will not be able to eliminate it completely. This may be distressing – we are suggesting that Access Review and Certification initiatives will never achieve absolute detective and preventive control on the organization's role engineering and evolution. However, as long as we keep the error arbitrarily small, these controls will work just fine, in theory at least.

Completing The Model: Closed Loop Feedback Control

To accomplish our control objective of Equation (4-9), we shall use classical feedback control (Siebert, 1986) whereby the Actual Authorization Roles Matrix is measured using an as yet unspecified sensor $S(x,t)$ and fed back to be compared to the reference via a comparator. The output of our overall feedback system is assigned the unknown $y(x,t)$.

The overall system is shows in Figure 4-3.

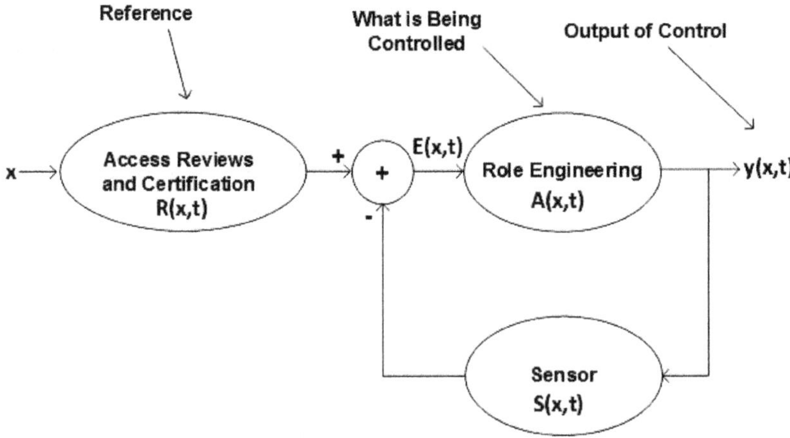

Figure 4-3: Closed Feedback Systems Engineering Model of IAM Controls.

While the theory of feedback control systems is wide and varied, we can show very simply that the model of Figure 4-3 serves our control objective of making sure that the Actual Roles Matrix is very nearly identical to the Reference Roles Matrix.

Focusing on the comparator junction, we can write at once after noting that the feedback is factoring in as a negative quantity,

$$E(x,t) = R(x,t) - S(x,t)y(x,t) \tag{4-10}$$

On the other hand, focusing on the forward loop

$$y(x,t) = A(x,t)E(x,t) \tag{4-11}$$

Solving for $E(x,t)$ in Equation (4-11) and substituting into Equation (4-10), we get

$$\frac{y(x,t)}{A(x,t)} = R(x,t) - S(x,t)y(x,t) \tag{4-12}$$

or

$$y(x,t) = \frac{A(x,t)}{1 + S(x,t)A(x,t)}R(x,t) \tag{4-13}$$

Equation (4-13) is a basic result from Systems Engineering and it has a simple but powerful application:

If we arrange the $S(x,t)$ *in such a way that*

$$|S(x,t)A(x,t)| \gg 1 \tag{4-14}$$

and

$$S(x,t) \approx 1 \tag{4-15}$$

then

$$y(x,t) \approx R(x,t) \tag{4-16}$$

In other words, we have succeeded in arranging for the output to be very nearly the same as the reference.

An Automated IAM Control Example

We previously evaluated the user's Roles Authorization Matrix whereby we quantized and reduced it to a binary scheme – see section *IAM Authorization System Interpretation*, Chapter 3. We were able to derive the Authorization Roles Matrix, thus, using Equation (3-41) or Equation (3-47), for some user x, we could write

$$y_{ij} = t_i(r_j x) \equiv t_i x + t_i r_j \tag{4-17}$$

or

$$y_{ij} = t_i(r_j x) = r_j t_i x + x t_i r_j \tag{4-18}$$

and eventually end up with, for example, the following assertion, Equation (3-46),

$$y_{ij} = \begin{cases} 1.0 \; if\ the\ user\ is\ authorized \\ 0.0 \; otherwise \end{cases} \tag{4-19}$$

Each such term represents an assertion to resource r_j by virtue of the user being assigned role t_i, and each user will have a complete set of these. We have termed it the Actual Authorization Roles Matrix in this section, Equation (4-20).

Let's now imagine a user with the following Actual Authorization Matrix

$$A(x_i, t) = \begin{bmatrix} 0 & 1 & 1 & 0 \\ 0 & 0 & 0 & 1 \\ 1 & 0 & 0 & 0 \\ 0 & 0 & 1 & 0 \\ 0 & 1 & 0 & 0 \end{bmatrix} \tag{4-20}$$

Next, let's assume the Reference Authorization Roles Matrix, $R(x_i, t)$ is as follows:

$$R(x_i, t) = \begin{bmatrix} 0 & 1 & 0 & 0 \\ 0 & 0 & 0 & 1 \\ 1 & 0 & 0 & 0 \\ 0 & 0 & 1 & 0 \\ 0 & 1 & 0 & 0 \end{bmatrix} \tag{4-21}$$

We believe our IAM Controls model offers the flexibility to define any number of controls, see section *A Modeling of IAM Controls* above for some examples. $A(x_i, t)$ above, for example, depicts a user who is assigned the role t_1 and the role is mapped to the resource r_3. However, per our detective and preventive control, $A(x_i, t)$, only users assigned role t_4 may access resource r_3, Figure 4-4.

$$A(\ldots) = \begin{bmatrix} t_1r_1 & t_1r_2 & t_1r_3 & t_1r_4 \\ t_2r_1 & t_2r_2 & t_2r_3 & t_2r_4 \\ t_3r_1 & t_3r_2 & t_3r_3 & t_3r_4 \\ t_4r_1 & t_4r_2 & t_4r_3 & t_4r_4 \\ t_5r_1 & t_5r_2 & t_5r_3 & t_5r_4 \end{bmatrix} \begin{bmatrix} 1 & 0 & \ldots & 0 \\ 0 & 1 & \ldots & \ldots \\ \ldots & \ldots & \ldots & \\ & & 1 & \ldots \\ 0 & 0 & \ldots & 1 \end{bmatrix} x_i$$

Figure 4-4: Detective and Preventive Controls: Assigned vs. Allowed.

To make further progress, we will make a transformation to Equations (4-20) and (4-21). Making transformations is an integral part of Systems Engineering modeling primarily because computation, conceptualization and even intuition is often easier in a domain other than the one where a particular engineering problem naturally presents itself. For example, in signals processing modeling, it is often easier to make a transformation from the time domain to the frequency domain. Once the problem is modeled and solved in the transformed domain, we may then transform it back and make our interpretation accordingly, or as many engineers will attest, sometimes it may be easier to perform everything from concept to design in the transformed domain. Engineering is a fantastic wonder!

We proceed in this spirit, thus, if we transform each row of Equations (4-20) and (4-21) to decimals, we get

$$A'(x_i, t) = \begin{bmatrix} 6 \\ 1 \\ 8 \\ 2 \\ 4 \end{bmatrix} \qquad \textbf{(4-22)}$$

where we have interpreted, for example, the first row as a stream of binary bits, 0110, which in decimal, according to a well-known binary to decimal conversion, equals

$$\begin{aligned} \mathbf{0\,1\,1\,0}\,(binary) &= \mathbf{0} * 2^3 + \mathbf{1} * 2^2 + \mathbf{1} * 2^1 + \mathbf{0} * 2^0 \\ &= 6\,(decimal) \end{aligned} \qquad \textbf{(4-23)}$$

Similarly,

$$R'(x_i, t) = \begin{bmatrix} 4 \\ 1 \\ 8 \\ 2 \\ 4 \end{bmatrix} \qquad \textbf{(4-24)}$$

We plot Equations (4-20) and (4-21) in Figure 4-5, noting that the only point of departure between the two in this simple example is the first row.

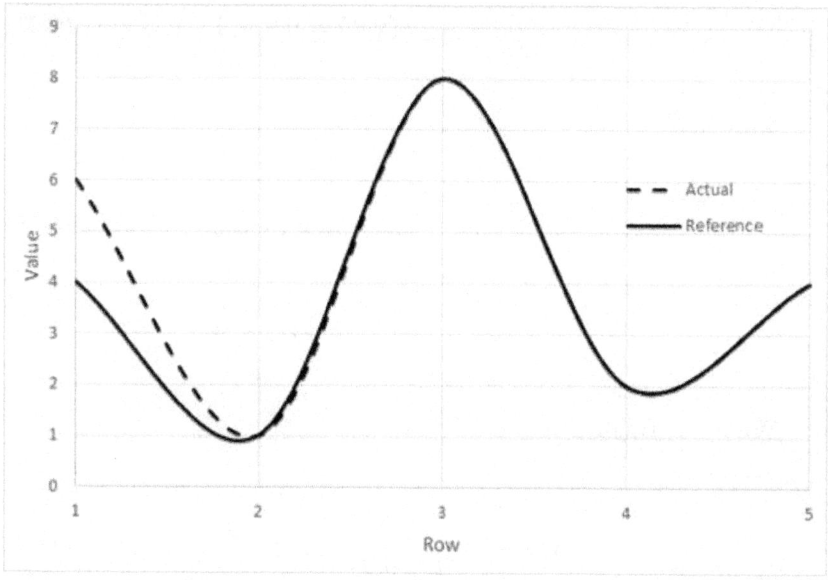

Figure 4-5: IAM Detective and Preventive Controls: Assigned vs. Reference Roles Authorization Matrix in Graphic Format.

Applying our model, Equations (4-13)-(4-15), and noting that Equation (4-13) may be applied to each row, one at a time, and choosing:

$$S(x,t) = 0.9 \qquad \textbf{(4-25)}$$

which is consistent with our two conditions, Equations (4-14) and (4-15),

$$|S(x,t)A(x,t)| = |0.9 * 6| = 5.4 \gg 1 \qquad \textbf{(4-26)}$$

and

$$S(x,t) = 0.9 \approx 1 \tag{4-27}$$

And since

$$A(x,t) = 6 \tag{4-28}$$

$$R(x,t) = 4 \tag{4-29}$$

We have, finally,

$$y(x,t) = \frac{6}{1 + 0.9 * 6} 4 = 3.75 \tag{4-30}$$

As can be seen from Equation (4-30), our simple model has provided significant corrective controls to the Roles Engineering output. What is more, the model outlined provides a framework for effective modeling of detective and preventive controls because, as can be easily see from Figure 4-5 and Figure 4-6, we may specify an arbitrary IAM Controls regime via the above transformation, and be able to control the results of our Role Engineering accordingly.

Note:

Even though we applied the model to a single point/row, Equation (4-30), *we could have easily applied it to all other rows. What is more, by converting the points into a smooth function of the row index, we can apply the model to an arbitrary number of points as* Figure 4-5 *suggests. We just have to be cautious to make sure that every point in the graph meets the two conditions of the model specified in* Equations (4-14) *and* (4-15)*. And we can easily make sure those conditions are met by, for example, shifting the curve up uniformly (by a constant).*

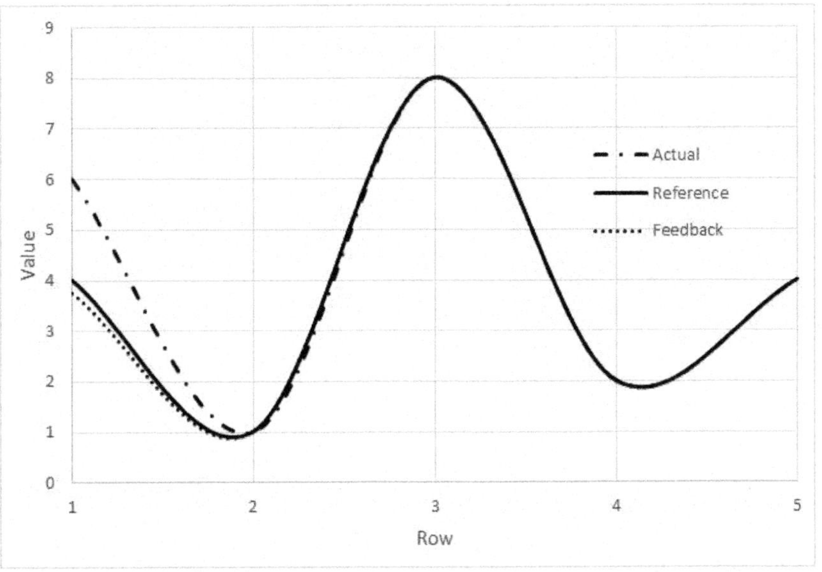

Figure 4-6: IAM Detective and Preventive Controls: Assigned vs. Reference vs. Feedback Corrected Roles Authorization Matrix.

SUMMARY

In this chapter we analyzed and modeled IAM Controls, specifically the IAM functions of Access Reviews and Certifications. The model key insights in this chapter are not only that we can model these seemingly human procedures and processes using simple ideas from Systems Engineering, but that we can do so in a very exact manner. The IAM controls models we created here may be used to apply arbitrary controls in any organization's Role Engineering process.

Chapter 5 - Trust Models in Identity and Access Management

INTRODUCTION

In 1556, Martin Guerre, a French peasant re-appeared in his village of Artigat in south west France after unexpectedly disappearing eight years earlier. He was re-united with his wife, Bertrande de Rols, the daughter of a prominent local family, and his now twenty year old son. Together again, the Guerre family soon celebrated the arrival of a second son and, soon thereafter a daughter (Davis, 1983).

For Bertrande, Martin's return was a huge blessing since the Catholic laws then in-force in France did not allow women who were so abandoned to remarry.

Meanwhile, the Guerre family suffered tragedies fairly common at the time. His new son died early in childhood and his father also passed away. Martin went ahead and inherited his father's property, perhaps too gladly so since it was a disagreement over some missing grain from the elder Guerre that had earlier been the trigger that precipitated Martin's abandonment of his family in 1548.

But Martin did not go far in his disappearance. He was actually alive and well in Spain, serving in the court of a cardinal there. Indeed, he even joined the army of the famous Spanish conquistador Pedro de Mendoza who sent him to Flanders, somewhere in present day France, Netherlands or Belgium. In Flanders, he was one of many foot soldiers in the Spanish army that attacked St. Quentin on August 10 of 1557. During that battle, Martin got wounded in the leg. His wounds proved very serious, and in fact one of his legs had to be amputated and replaced with a wooden prosthetic.

After he got healed, he worked odd jobs in another Spanish monastery before returning to Artigat, perhaps because he was now feeling more vulnerable than before his journey to Spain.

Soon after his return, however, a battle started brewing between Martin, Betrande, and Martin's four sisters and uncles on the one hand, and one Pierre Guerre (*there* is a relation) and other villagers on the other. Pierre was Martin's new step father, having earlier married Martin's widowed mother during the latter's absence. Pierre and the villagers believed Martin was an impostor since a soldier who had fought alongside Martin in Spain passed through Artigat during his travails and believed that the real Martin had a wooden leg.

The conflict raged on, with Bertrande siding with her husband and Pierre and her sons-in-law going as far as assaulting Martin with clubs.

It all came to a head in 1559 in a court face-off whereby Martin was charged with impersonation and arson. The case was disposed of in 1590 with Martin getting acquitted, perhaps on the strength of Bertrande's own testimony, for which jury would sit in judgment otherwise when the wife was sticking with her husband who had left a mere one decade earlier?

Pierre was however not one to give up easily. He applied heavy pressure on Bertrande to change her testimony and did further research into his 'prodigal' step son's background, including a visit to the neighboring village of Sajas. Ultimately, Pierre convinced the local authorities to institute a new case against Martin in 1560 at Rieux.

During the new trial, Bertrande intimated that she had initially believed that Martin was her real husband, but had since believed otherwise based on new information, mostly from Pierre. Not to be outdone, Martin testified about their life together before he disappeared, accounts of which matched those of Bertrande's. In fact, Martin challenged Betrande that if she could swear that he was not her real husband, he would gladly agree to be executed – not an empty bluff since impersonation was a capital offense in 16th century France. Bertrande was silent on the face of that challenge.

After a parade of over 150 witnesses, and despite Bertrande's equivocation in the face of Martin's self-immolation, Martin Guerre was nevertheless found guilty of all charges and sentenced to death.

Staring at the prospects of a date with the hangman's noose, Martin had to think fast. (In case the reader is wondering why a noose is being used in 16th century France, he must be instructed that Dr. Joseph-Ignace Guillotin had not yet invented his life's work; in fact, it would be another 178 years before the famous doctor would be born). Martin appealed to the highest court of the land – the French parliamentary assembly at Toulouse. He so eloquently presented his defense, based largely on allegations of subornation of perjury on the part of Pierre that the judges tended to believe his story. Indeed, Pierre was arrested and charged with subornation of perjury for allegedly pressuring Bertrande to commit perjury for greedy financial gain. Bertrande herself was also arrested and charged with perjury ('on a charge of false accusation' as it was then referred to).

Martin endured a grueling questioning about his past, details of which were checked and cross checked without any contradictions being discovered. Martin's case, however, fell apart when another man appeared, complete with a wooden leg, and who was able to answer to many more details about Martin Guerre's past than Martin himself could. Realizing his case was lost, Martin confessed to the judges about his real identity: Arnaud du Tilh from the village of Sajas. The judges then quickly affirmed his death sentence on September 12 1560, the judgment reportedly being witnessed by, among others, one Michel du Montaigne, who later became one of the most influential French renaissance writers.

After apologizing to all involved, including Bertrande, and

revealing that his fraud was triggered by constantly being confused for Martin Guerre, Arnaud was promptly hanged on September 16, 1560.

Human Trust, System Trust

Trust is very integral to human existence and experience. It is often said that we would never do such basic things as sitting down on chair if we did not have trust embedded deep inside our DNA. Without trust, even small details of our daily existence would be terrifying, and we would spend most of our time constantly verifying every little action or object, instead of going about our lives.

But the case of Arnaud de Tilh is a cautionary tale of the perils of human trust. Regardless of what Bertrande's motivations were – (Davis, 1983) argues that the limits put on women at the time forced Bertrande to silently conspire with Arnaud since she needed a husband, while Finlay believes she was genuinely duped (Finlay, 1988) – it is a powerful reminder of the pervasive role that trust plays in our human existence.

In IAM, we are mostly interested in System Trust. But there is a big Human Trust component as well since many System "Trust Vectors" are either initiated by or pass through human processes.

Human Trust is very automatic and is based on factors that are indeed very hard for computer systems to understand. Face recognition, for example, is fairly easy for humans, Bertrande de Rols notwithstanding. So is voice recognition. And in the larger animal kingdom, trust may be based on smell, touch and even taste.

It seems as if the ease with which Human Trust flows forth is only matched by the ease with which it may be thwarted or otherwise compromised. From the infamous cons in finance (Charles Ponzi and Robert Madoff are famous examples) to religious cons to the vast arena of political fraud, human trust is susceptible to all kinds of breaches. These breaches cut across educational background, social class and other sophistication.

In 1995, it became public that Mark Whitacre, PhD, the President of Archer Daniels Midland's BioProducts Division, had been acting as an FBI informant for a period of time. Archer Daniels Midland or ADM, an American agro-business conglomerate, was at the time unknowingly under investigation of the United States Federal Government authorities for anti-competitive price fixing schemes.

At about the same time, confident artists in the West African country of Nigeria came up with a simple yet ingenious scheme to separate Americans and other Westerners from their money. The scammer would pretend to be the relative of a wealthy but a corrupt government official who had recently died or otherwise fell out of favor with the local authorities. Then there would be a little matter of a large sum of money needing to be transferred out of the country to a safe location abroad, but only if a relatively smaller facilitating bank fee were available from the scammed. For their trouble, the scammed was promised a sizable share of the loot.

After the initial bank fee had been wired to the scam artist, several other 'fees' would be requested to 'complete' the transaction, one after the other. For Dr. Whitacre, these fees eventually added up to several million dollars, all of which came from ADM's corporate accounts. A fascinating account of this tale is recounted by Kurt Eichenwald in his best seller corporate finance thriller *The Informant* (Eichenwald, 2000).

Then there is the human trust of authority, especially one in uniform. It is relatively easy to impersonate a uniformed official, including a police officer. Human beings are trained to recognize the uniform and immediately make the connection between the uniform and the authority behind it. This has led to criminals impersonating police officers, Salvation Army collection agents, and bank web sites, among other valuable information.

Computer System Trust has struggled to emulate the facility by which humans evaluate and establish trust. For example, elementary problems for humans like face recognition are still a challenge to computers despite tremendous progress in artificial intelligence and computer vision in recent years. Indeed computer trust seems to be captured quite aptly by the famous dog cartoon by Peter Steiner (Figure 5-1).

"On the Internet, nobody knows you're a dog."

Figure 5-1: "On the Internet, nobody knows you're a dog", © Peter Steiner.

Establishment and propagation of computer trust will occupy the rest of this chapter, beginning with the laying of the boundaries of our topic next.

Risk and Uncertainty in IAM Systems

In IAM, we are mostly concerned with the intersection of Computer System Trust, Human Trust and the related Process Trust. We will not cover the larger topic of Human Trust; instead we will capture and attempt to model all elements of Human Trust into Organization Processes.

But what exactly is Trust in the IAM context?

Trust is action in the face of uncertain risk.

As one author puts it,

> *"Trust is a risky investment. The actor who trusts runs risks. He trusts that his expectations will be fulfilled. Although he has no certainty whatsoever, he acts as if everything he expects and trusts in will, in fact, come true" (Luhman 1989).*

Human Trust is actually easier to attain in a sense since we can make some judgments regarding the risky situations and make tradeoffs between different them. For example, before purchasing a copy of Tolstoy's *War and Peace* when it was first released in 1865, the purchaser would probably tether his horse and carriage at the local book seller. The book seller was probably a well-known personality or at least a well-established brick and mortar edifice very similar to their 21st century counterparts. The purchaser would probably then walk in and browse the book, portions of which they would already be familiar with from newspaper excerpts or serialization. The purchaser would then hand the book seller cash (or gold as the case may have been) and receive the book in return.

All along the process, the purchaser would have several "trust cues", including perhaps the book itself being leather bound, indicating to the purchase that many years of literary enjoyment lay ahead.

Contrast that to a 21st century writer ordering the same book online. The purchaser would power up their laptop computer or app, login and connect to some kind of wide area network like the Internet. Even before the purchaser can access the book retailer's web site, they would have already interacted with several sophisticated systems whose operation the purchaser is unlikely to be much familiar with, let alone understand, and thus they must trust lest they be stopped cold before powering up their computing device.

These include:

- *The Computer, Laptop or Tablet – a general purpose computer, which is one of the most sophisticated machines ever invented by man, and whose operation the actor most likely takes on a faith (trust) basis.*

- *Computer Software, Application or "App" – The operating system software alone may have perhaps 50 million lines of code. Even if we use modular systems abstraction, it is almost impossible for any human being to use such software without placing a healthy dose of trust that it will behave correctly.*

- *The Connective Internetwork (Internet) – Most users of public networks like the Internet simply trust that it will work when they connect to it. The actual operation of the Internet is complex and full of intrigue, and even sophisticated users with technical knowledge of the underlying operations of the Internet have to resort to trust for the most part.*

One may argue that we trust the computer since we have seen it work correctly in the past. Or that we trust it based on the trust that its developers place on it, such that their trust becomes our own.

These are both true statements, but only to an extent. First of all, our trust of Computer Systems (or more generally, technology), is only partially based on prior experience with the technology since most users have experienced catastrophic events blamed on technology or have seen others succumb to technology's many foibles, be it a laptop computer catching fire or the Space Shuttle exploding.

These failures of technology force us to resort to Trust, as opposed to actual knowledge, in our interaction with technology-based products. It is for this reason that many airplane travelers have it at the back of their minds, however far behind that is, that the plane they are now boarding may not actually reach its destination before falling off the skies or sliding off the runway.

On an even more fundamental level, technology developers and operators have come to the conclusion that however perfectly designed a technological system is, it is impossible to anticipate all constellations of the system beyond a trivial enumeration of its finite states (Denning et. al, 1997). Without this ability, they cannot guarantee an error prone operation even if all constituent parts of the system performed flawlessly. We believe this is merely a restatement of the fundamental uncertainty principle as it applies to technical systems.

In other words, risk and uncertainty are a fundamental property of nature, including the systems we model here. In our treatment of IAM Systems, we will treat Risk (and, analogously, Uncertainty) as a property of a system that participating co-systems have to factor in before the overall IAM System trust may be derived.

Modeling Risk & Uncertainty in IAM Systems

Our starting point towards a model of Risk in IAM systems is the User Security Context, which we depicted in Chapter 2.

As you may recall, we represented Authentication as a convolution of the user supplied credentials with the stored User Credentials Store, Equation (2-21), which we copy below:

$$y[n] = \sum_{m=0}^{m=n} \vec{x}[n-m] * \vec{c}[m] \qquad \textbf{(5-1)}$$

An authenticated user then proceeds through an authorization process where they receive a set of assertions represented by the following model, Equation (3-39), also reproduced below:

$$\begin{bmatrix} y_{11} & y_{12} & \cdots & y_{1n} \\ y_{21} & y_{22} & \cdots & \cdots \\ \cdots & \cdots & \cdots & \\ & & y_{ij} & \cdots \\ y_{m1} & y_{m2} & \cdots & y_{mn} \end{bmatrix} = \begin{bmatrix} t_1r_1 & t_1r_2 & \cdots & t_1r_n \\ t_2r_1 & t_2r_2 & \cdots & \cdots \\ \cdots & \cdots & \cdots & \\ & & t_ir_j & \cdots \\ t_mr_1 & t_mr_1 & \cdots & t_mr_n \end{bmatrix} \begin{bmatrix} 1 & 0 & \cdots & 0 \\ 0 & 1 & \cdots & \cdots \\ \cdots & \cdots & \cdots & \\ & & 1 & \cdots \\ 0 & 0 & \cdots & 1 \end{bmatrix} x_i \qquad \textbf{(5-2)}$$

We may recast Equation (5-2) as follows, by abstracting out the details of the authorization process

$$A(x_l, t) = \begin{bmatrix} t_1r_1 & t_1r_2 & \dots & t_1r_n \\ t_2r_1 & t_2r_2 & \dots & \dots \\ \dots & \dots & \dots & \\ & & t_ir_j & \dots \\ t_mr_1 & t_mr_1 & \dots & t_mr_n \end{bmatrix} \begin{bmatrix} 1 & 0 & \dots & 0 \\ 0 & 1 & \dots & \dots \\ \dots & \dots & \dots & \\ & & 1 & \dots \\ 0 & 0 & \dots & 1 \end{bmatrix} x_l \quad \textbf{(5-3)}$$

Equation (5-3) represents the User's assertions token that will be consumed by all backend applications that come after the IAM Authenticator and IAM Authorizer.

We have introduced time dependence here since in general, assertions are time dependent (e.g. period or time-limited), and x_l represents the user.

We represent the propagation of Post-Authentication and Post-Authorization Trust visually as follows, Figure 5-2:

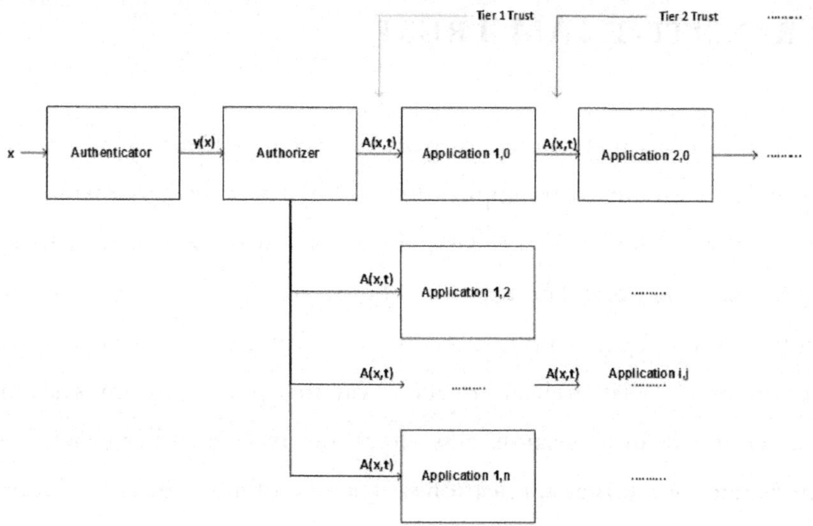

Figure 5-2: Propagation of IAM Trust.

In Figure 5-2 we have divided each application (or component) according to their 'application' distance from the Authorizer. *Application i,j*, for example, is *i* applications removed from the Authorizer, meaning it is potentially faced with the possibility of consuming an assertion that has been 'handed down' *(i-1)* times.

Furthermore, Figure 5-2 does not yet make any assumptions regarding the nature of propagation; it only shows how IAM Trust may propagate from one sub-component to another. We have also not considered cross-index trust, i.e. *Application i,j* trusting Assertions from *Application i,j-1*, etc. This is only a simplifying assumption since Figure 5-2 potentially represents an $n \times m$ trust network.

How Trust propagation may happen more precisely is the subject of the following sections.

TRANSITIVE IAM TRUST

Applications may choose to trust the Security Context presented to them by the upstream application simply based on possession. In other words, *Application i,j* trusts the assertion token received from *Application i-1, j* etc. The trust may be based on the enterprise-wide understanding by the application architect that there is an established Perimeter of Trust firewall in such a way that practically any session that contains an Assertion must have received it either from the Authorizer or another application with a direct line to the Authorizer.

This type of IAM Trust is called Transitive Trust since there is no requirement that the application validate any assertion it receives from an up-stream application. The Application trusts that its up-stream counterpart has already validated the Assertion. Applying this logic recursively, the chain of trust eventually ends at the Authorizer as the ultimate source of IAM Authorization System trust.

Transitive Trust in IAM is fairly useful, if somewhat risky. In an IAM System with many applications or sub-systems, it becomes very cumbersome for each such component to verify the security context since such verification must be done with every request for it to be valid (if the verification were not done with each request, it is presumable that a malicious actor may simply detect the timeslots when the verification does not happen, and then defeat the system by replaying the correct security context accordingly).

Closed Loop IAM Trust

We may also imagine a situation whereby each time an application receives an assertion, it checks it with the Authorizer to make sure the assertion is still valid. We depict such a closed loop IAM Trust as follows:

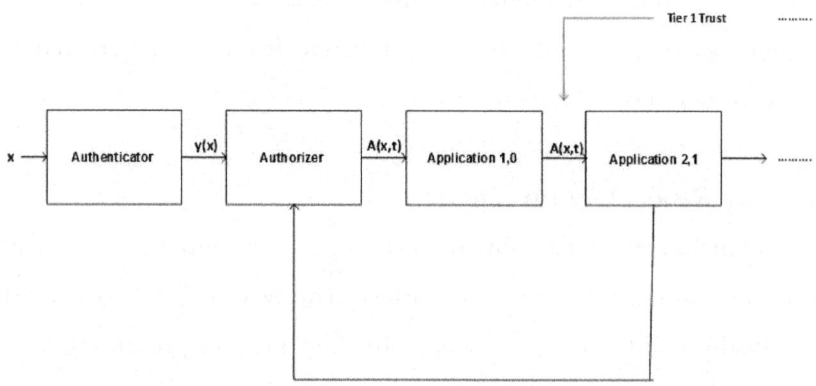

Figure 5-3: Closed Loop IAM Trust

The Closed Loop IAM Trust eliminates many risks that may be associated with a user's assertion since the assertion is checked against perhaps the place where it is most likely to be accurate, namely the Authorizer (which, as a matter of self-consistency, must keep track all the assertions it has issued).

The previous sentence implies that even the Authorizer may not have the correct assertion for the current user. We say this because there are several factors that may affect the accuracy of the stored assertion. Some of these are listed below. Note that we are less concerned about mitigating these risks than the fact that there is a non-zero (or non-trivial possibility that the stated risk will occur):

Transport Risks

The assertion may be compromised en-route from the Authorizer to the Authorizer's store.

Storage Risks

The Assertion may have been created correctly, but compromised after being stored. An application that checks for its validity will then be given a compromised Assertion, different from the one created by the legitimate user.

Larceny Risks (Identity Theft)

A malicious user may obtain a valid user's credentials and present it to our Authenticator and Authorizer. The resulting Assertions are technically valid since they were obtained via the presentation of valid credentials, but they don't represent their duly authorized owner.

Systemic Risks

It is entirely possible that a configuration or even a programming error could result in an incorrect assertion. The resulting assertion is perhaps in the worst of all situations since the user thinks they have a valid assertion and the IAM System also believes the assertion is correct.

In the face of all these uncertainties, it is apparent that any assertion received must be treated as suspect.

Uncertainty in IAM

Uncertainty (or risk) is a difficult and fascinating topic. It has been with us since times immemorial. Indeed, the only certain statement we can make about uncertainty is that it is certain to happen. At some point. We illustrate this below.

As told by Peter Bernstein (Bernstein, 1998), one winter night during a particularly brutal German air raids on Moscow during the Second World War, a distinguished Soviet professor of statistics showed up in his local air-raid shelter. He had never appeared there before.

"There are 7 million people in Moscow," he was heretofore known to say.

"Why should I expect them to hit me?"

His friends were therefore astonished to see him and asked what had happened to change his mind.

"Look," he explained, "there are seven million people in Moscow and one elephant. Last night they got the elephant!"

About the same time, and long before he won the Nobel Prize in Economics, Kenneth J. Arrow was a weather forecaster for the US Air Force. Some officers had been assigned the task of forecasting the weather one month ahead of time, but when they consulted with

Arrow and his fellow statisticians, the officers were told that such long range forecasts were no better than random numbers pulled out of a hat.

The forecasters agreed and asked their superiors to be relieved of this duty. The reply came back very swiftly:

"The Commanding General is well aware that the forecasts are no good. However, he needs them for planning purposes." (Ibid).

Risk is the science of chance. For our purposes, we shall keep things very simple, and we will use only the most elementary ideas of this science.

§§

We will begin by positing that any time an Assertion is presented to an IAM component or application, the validity of that assertion will be in question and we cannot guarantee that it is being presented for the correct user. Indeed, the same statement may also be made about the initial authentication process, as well as the sub-sequent authorizations.

To start our model, we shall review very briefly some elementary concepts regarding modeling of events of chance using a much simplified example of the business of car insurance.

CAR INSURANCE

Many countries have some laws that mandate that everyone purchase insurance for their motor vehicle. Such insurance is essentially a bet against the risk of an accident happening during a particular period of time (policy duration).

But what exactly is risk? How does the insurance company set the rates for different types of risk?

In order for the insurance company to break even, all they need to do is determine, on average, how often accidents occur in the pool of drivers that they cover. If, for example, the insurance company knows that, in the coming year, seven hundred and fifty (750) of their 10,000 customers in their area of coverage will get involved in an accident, and that each of these accidents will cost the insurance company on average $1500 (after deductibles of course), then the insurance company may determine their position as follows:

$$Next\ Year's\ Payouts = 750 * 1500 = \$1{,}125{,}000 \qquad \textbf{(5-4)}$$

If the next year turns out exactly like the insurance company thought it would, then assuming the firm simply wants to break even, there are no ancillary costs associated with providing the insurance (like administrative costs, etc), and that the insurance company puts the premium collected in a bank account that earns exactly an interest rate equal to the average inflation for the next year, then the insurance company should charge each of its customer's a premium equal to its cost spread across all those insured:

$$Insurance\ Premium = \frac{Cost}{\#\ of\ Insured} = \frac{\$1{,}125{,}000}{10{,}000} = \$112.50 \tag{5-5}$$

At the end of the year, i.e. after collecting its premiums and paying out all the above losses, the insurance firm calculates its risk for the past year as

$$Last\ Year's\ Risk = \frac{\#\ of\ Accidents}{\#\ of\ Vehicles} = \frac{750}{10{,}000} = 0.075 \tag{5-6}$$

Note that the insurance company divides the total number of accidents by the total number of cars since insuring 10,000 cars in the county possibly means all 10,000 cars may be in an accident during any given year – the insurance company argues this possibility exists, albeit remotely so.

Additionally, we notice that Equation (5-6) represents the *probability* of *any one car* having an accident during the past year, and is referred to as an after-the-fact or *a posteriori* probability. Once the insurance company has determined this probability, they can simply calculate the premium for *any* driver by multiplying it by the expected cost of each car that gets into an accident:

$$Premium = Risk * Expected\ Cost = 0.075 * 1500 = \$112.50 \tag{5-7}$$

Unfortunately for the insurance company, however, they have to set the rates at the *beginning* of the year, i.e. before the accidents start occurring. What the insurance firm needs to do is *predict* ahead of time the probability that any particular car will have an accident, i.e. *a priori* probability.

This is obviously a much simplified picture of the actual reality of car insurance, but the reader may appreciate that the insurance company has a lot resting on predicting the *a priori* probability as accurately as they can possibly do it; if it underestimates the risk, the firm risks depleting its capital paying claims without collecting adequate premium (and if it overestimates the risk, it risks losing market share or, in regulated markets, going over the mandated level) Indeed, insurance firms sometimes collapse under a flood of claims from insurable natural disasters like hurricanes or floods, for example.

Coming up with *a priori* probability is a fairly sophisticated task, and we will not attempt it here, but we note that insurance companies spend a lot of resources calculating *a priori* probabilities and have codified it in a profession called *actuarial sciences*.

IAM PROBABILITIES

In Identity and Access Management, uncertainty occurs despite technology's great strides in message assurance and authenticity. Breaches happen often and frequently. The result is that any assertion (or even authentication) is suspect, and truly has but a degree of certainty even when correct credentials are presented.

In other words, the probability that a user is not who they say they are is non-zero and represents systemic risk to the firm. It is also possible that a user is who they say they are, but the assertions they hold do not belong to them.

To illustrate what we mean, we will start with our authentication result from Chapter 2, Equation (2-22), which we repeat below:

$$y[n] = \sum_{m=0}^{m=n} \vec{a}_l * \vec{b}_n * \delta[l-m] * \delta[m] \tag{5-8}$$

Note that Equation (5-8) represents a single user authenticating, and is the view of a single user interacting with the IAM System. In modeling risk, however, it is more appropriate to consider the entire user population (just like the car insurance company considers the entire pool of insured clients), and come up with gross statistics, again, similar in spirit to the case of a car insurance company.

Thus, suppose there are n users in the IAM System. We may represent their authentication states at any given time using the following vector:

$$\begin{bmatrix} y[1,t] \\ \dots \\ y[i,t] \\ \dots \\ y[n,t] \end{bmatrix} = Authentication\ State\ at\ time\ t \qquad \textbf{(5-9)}$$

Equation (5-9) is nothing more than a statement of the authentication state of the IAM System. We may think of the vector as representing all users who are currently authenticated to the IAM System at some time t. We have introduced time dependence since authentication state is of course generally time-dependent.

Equation (5-9) represents multiple users who are in different authentication states. Some of them may be authenticated and thus have active sessions. Other states may contain users who are not logged in to the IAM System (so they don't possess any Authentication context at all). Yet other users may have recently logged in with a bad password several times resulting in an account lockout, etc.

Regardless of the actual Authentication states represented in Equation (5-9), we may assign a risk to the Authentication state vector by the following conjectures regarding the property of such risk to the IAM system:

- There will exist multiple independent types of risk (or more accurately, Risk Vectors) in the IAM System. These will in general have different risk characteristic, and may include, for example, risk from phishing attacks, those from shared credentials, and yet others from identity theft via social engineering or even those from Trojan horse type of computer viruses.

- There is a distinct and real possibility for the risk to spread from one user to other users as the risk evolves over time. This is the general nature of IAM threat vectors since it maximizes the potential illicit gains of malicious attacker.

> *These are the two major properties of IAM risk that we now model. There are certainly other properties, but perhaps not as pervasive in their effect on the overall systemic risk as these two. For example, within a risk type, there exists a generally time-dependent risk evolution. In other words, the "level of risk" of the threat will evolve over time. Such evolution does not always exist, but when it does, it means the risk level will most likely either increase as the malicious (or benevolent) actors gain the upper hand or decrease as counter-measures are applied. We do not model this behavior except to note that each term in Figure 5-4 below is time dependent.*

To conform to these properties, each risk type has to be represented by a matrix of risks, with the diagonal components representing points of risk origination and off-diagonal components representing risk propagation from other users. We illustrate this below.

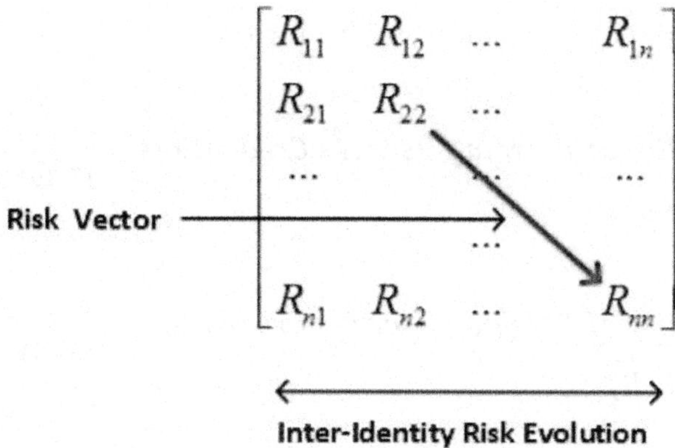

Figure 5-4: Risk Vector Propagation

Figure 5-4, diagonal terms represent the probability of the risk type occurring to some user while the off diagonal terms of represent the chances that the same risk type will spread to this user as demonstrated below.

Still modeling just one risk type, to get the risk adjusted authentication result for all users, it is useful to consider a very simple case first.

§§

Suppose that we have only two users in our IAM system, User A and User B. Furthermore, let's consider just one risk type of identity theft via phishing.

We denote the probability of User A suffering an identity theft via a phishing attack as P(A), and similarly, P(B) for User B.

$$\begin{aligned} &Event\ A\text{: } Probability\ of\ Phishing\ User\ A's\ Credentials \\ &\quad = P(A) \end{aligned} \tag{5-10}$$

$$\begin{aligned} &Event\ B\text{: } Probability\ of\ Phishing\ User\ B's\ Credentials \\ &\quad = P(B) \end{aligned} \tag{5-11}$$

We are also interested in a third event, namely the probability that the risk spreads from one user to the other. Given the nature of IAM Systems, this is a real possibility that may not be ignored:

$$\begin{aligned} &Event\ C\text{: } Probability\ of\ Phishing\ Attack\ Spreading \\ &\quad From\ One\ User\ to\ the\ Other = P(S) \end{aligned} \tag{5-12}$$

For simplicity, we assume that this is independent of the user, but may depend on the type of risk.

(Note that the following treatment uses some elementary/fundamental properties of probabilities from Probability Theory)

§§

(1)

First, the events defined above are trigged by a user's authentication. Since an authentication result is generally binary, Equation (2-9),

$$y[n] = \begin{cases} 1, n = l \\ 0, n \neq l \end{cases} \quad \textbf{(5-13)}$$

by introducing risk, we are essentially removing this binary property of authentication and instead replacing its binary value with a range of possibilities between 0 and 1 depending on the risk attached to it.

For example, we will define the risk adjusted authentication state simply as

$$y'[n, t] = P(\dots) * y[n. t] \quad \textbf{(5-14)}$$

In Equation (5-14), $P(\dots)$ is the risk factor (derived below) that represents our uncertainty regarding whether the authentication is valid or not. As an example, Equation (5-14) may 'adjust' Equation (5-13) to:

$$y[n] = \begin{cases} 0.995, n = l \\ 0.000, n \neq l \end{cases} \quad \textbf{(5-15)}$$

Equation (5-15) means that, to the best of our knowledge, of which we are 99.5% assured, the user authentication in question is valid. Conversely, it says we think there is a 0.5% chance that the authentication is not valid as far as we know (for example, someone may be impersonating the true identity).

In Equation (5-15), *we note that for* $n \neq l$, *the value is still zero because this represents all comparisons of the users credentials with other credentials in the credentials store. Because we have assumed user IDs to be unique in the credentials store, it is not possible to find a match at other locations other than* $n = l$ *because those locations will not match on the user ID basis.*

It is certainly possible that an intruder will impersonate a valid user, but we will model that in $P(\ldots)$, *and apply it to the uncertainty at* $n = l$ *per Equation (5-15).*

For a user who is not logged in (either legitimately or via a malicious denial of service action), it is assumed that Equation (5-15) equals to a number close to zero (but non-zero due to the uncertainty surrounding our knowledge of their authentication status) – Equation (5-16), for example:

$$y'[n] = \begin{cases} 0.001, n = l \\ 0.000, n \neq l \end{cases} \tag{5-16}$$

This is not an undue restriction as we shall see shortly.

(2)

Second, we assume that Event A and Event B are independent. This is a safe assumption in this case because in real life, phishing attacks on different users will be independent of each other.

(3)

Third, we are interested in calculating the systemic risk that a phishing attack on one or both users will cause. From above, we know that once User B's credentials are compromised by the attack, then it is possible that User A's credentials may also be compromised. The resulting compromise on User A will most likely not be a phishing attack, but another attack vector (type) entirely. Nevertheless, its origin will have been the original Phishing attack of User B.

§§

From User A's perspective, the risk experienced may come from one of two events occurring:

EITHER

{**Event 1** = *User A's Authentication Session becomes subject of a phishing attack*}

OR

{**Event 2** = *User B's Authentication Session becomes subject of a phishing attack.*

AND

Event 3 = *Risk spreads from User B to User A*}

(Relationship 1)

To keep things simple, we will ignore the event where both User A and User B become subjects of independent phishing attacks for now. However, this and perhaps other scenarios are also easily amenable to the analysis that follows.

Note I:

Event 2 and Event 3 are dependent, but Event 1 is independent of the combination of Events 2 & Event 3.

Note II:

We have ignored the scenario whereby both users are the subjects of an identity borne attack and the risk spreads from User B to User A. This assumption makes our model (more) risk averse, and is consistent with what an IAM security system should be.

We may then simply express the above probabilities as follows, Equation (5-10) above:

$$Probability(Event\ 1) = P(A) \quad \textbf{(5-17)}$$

And,

$$Probability(Event\ 2\ and\ Event\ 3) = P(S/B)P(B) \quad \textbf{(5-18)}$$

In Equation (5-18), we have used the bar notation from elementary Probability Theory. It is called *conditional probability*, i.e. the probability of one event given the fact that some other event has occurred.

$P(S/B)$ *is read as the probability that event* S *occurs given that event* S *has occurred.*

From Probability Theory, we know that the probability of any two events, Event x OR Event y, may be expressed as:

$$P(x \ or \ y) = P(x) + P(y) - P(x \ and \ y) \quad \textbf{(5-19)}$$

Also, conditional probability of Event x occurring given that another Event y has occurred may be expressed as follows:

$$P(x/y) = \frac{P(x \ and \ y)}{P(y)} \quad \textbf{(5-20)}$$

§§

Using Equations (5-19) and (5-20), we may write the expression for User A's risk, reproduced below,

EITHER

{***Event 1*** = *User A's Authentication Session becomes subject of a phishing attack*}

OR

{***Event 2*** = *User B's Authentication Session becomes subject of a phishing attack.*

AND

Event 3 = *Risk spreads from User B to User A*}.

(Relationship 1)

as follows

$$Probability(\{Event\ 1\}\ or\ \{Event\ 2\ and\ Event\ 3\}) \\ = P(A) + P(S/B)P(B) \\ - P(Event\ 1\ and\ \{Event\ 2\ and\ Event\ 3\}) \qquad (5\text{-}21)$$

In Equation (5-21), we may use the following relationship for independent events:

$$P(A\ and\ B) = P(A)P(B)\ \ A\ and\ B\ independent \qquad \textbf{(5-22)}$$

to rewrite the last term as

$$P(Event\ 1\ and\ \{Event\ 2\ and\ Event\ 3\}) = P(A)P(S/B)P(B) \qquad \textbf{(5-23)}$$

The risk to User A's authentication from phishing is then expressed as:

$$P_A(A) = P(A) + P(S/B)P(B) - P(A)P(S/B)P(B) \qquad \textbf{(5-24)}$$

Equation (5-24) may be simplified by noticing that the last term is expected to be significantly smaller than the other two:

- $P(A)$ and $P(B)$ are most likely going to be of the same order or not significantly different in terms of magnitude because when dealing with a large population, there is no reason *a priori* to assume that the phishing risks for one user will differ significantly from another. Admittedly, there would be conditions where this assumption is not tenable; for example, where one user has their device's more security updated than the rest; nonetheless this is an assumption going into the model.

Note however that the assumption only allows us to derive closed form results below; the full model may be used without this assumption.

- $P(S/B)$ is perhaps expected to be on the same order of $P(A)$ and $P(B)$, therefore the last term of Equation (5-24) may be dropped, thus:

$$P_A(A) \approx P(A) + P(S/B)P(B) \tag{5-25}$$

We may formally define the conditions when Equation (5-25) is valid, namely

$$P(A)P(S/B)P(B) \ll P(A) + P(S/B)P(B) \tag{5-26}$$

or

$$\frac{P(A)P(S/B)P(B)}{P(A) + P(S/B)P(B)} \ll 1 \tag{5-27}$$

With this approximation, we may write User A's risk adjusted authentication state as follows, noting that the first term is tied to the user A's login and the second to User B's:

$$y'[A,t] = P(A)y[A,t] + P(S/B)P(B)y[B,t] \tag{5-28}$$

Similarly, we find that the risk adjusted authentication status for User B is

$$y'[B,t] = P(B)y[B,t] + P(S/A)P(A)y[A,t] \tag{5-29}$$

Putting Equations (5-28) and (5-29) in matrix or system form, we get

$$\begin{bmatrix} y'[A,t] \\ y'[B,t] \end{bmatrix} = \begin{bmatrix} P(A) & P(S/B)P(B) \\ P(S/A)P(A) & P(B) \end{bmatrix} \begin{bmatrix} y[A,t] \\ y[B,t] \end{bmatrix} \tag{5-30}$$

In Engineering Physics, Equation (5-30) has a natural symmetry that is beautiful to look at. We will interpret is below.

§§

The steps leading from Equation (5-14), repeated below:

$$y'[n,t] = P(\ldots) * y[n.t] \quad \textbf{(5-31)}$$

to Equation (5-28) through Equation (5-30), also below:

$$y'[A,t] = P(A)y[A,t] + P(S/B)P(B)y[B,t] \quad \textbf{(5-32)}$$

$$y'[B,t] = P(B)y[B,t] + P(S/A)P(A)y[A,t] \quad \textbf{(5-33)}$$

$$\begin{bmatrix} y'[A,t] \\ y'[B,t] \end{bmatrix} = \begin{bmatrix} P(A) & P(S/B)P(B) \\ P(S/A)P(A) & P(B) \end{bmatrix} \begin{bmatrix} y[A,t] \\ y[B,t] \end{bmatrix} \quad \textbf{(5-34)}$$

may seem like a sleight of hand. Indeed, algebraically, Equation (5-32) should instead be written as follows, in light of Equation (5-31):

$$y'[A,t] = \{P(A) + P(S/B)P(B)\}y[A,t] \quad \textbf{(5-35)}$$

Our argument here is that in Equation (5-25),

$$P_A(A) \approx P(A) + P(S/B)P(B) \quad \textbf{(5-36)}$$

the first term is tied to User A's authentication while the second term is derived from User B's authentication state, making Equation (5-32) the more correct model of the underlying process. Indeed, if we use the full form of the result in Equation (5-24),

$$P_A(A) = P(A) + P(S/B)P(B) - P(A)P(S/B)P(B) \qquad \textbf{(5-37)}$$

the third term may be recognized as the result of the both authentication processes. This is the 'higher order' term that we discarded in the approximation leading to Equation (5-25) on the basis that the product probabilities will be comparatively smaller than individual probabilities.

Another viewpoint is that there is no theoretical difficulty in forming the following Risk Matrix System,

$$R = \begin{bmatrix} P(A) & P(S/B)P(B) \\ P(S/A)P(A) & P(B) \end{bmatrix} \qquad \textbf{(5-38)}$$

and analyzing its properties, independently of the algebraic equations above because each element of the system (or matrix) is well defined according to the elements of Equation (5-36). Such a matrix tells us something about the systemic IAM risk, and once its properties are understood, we can apply it to any user according to the algebraic relation in Equation (5-36).

In the following analysis, we take both views; first one for algebraic convenience and the second for its more rigorous foundation.

§§

The above Authentication Risk Matrix may be applied to the entire user population, yielding, for one type of risk and subject to the linearized approximation above:

$$\begin{bmatrix} y'[1,t] \\ \dots \\ y'[i,t] \\ \dots \\ y'[n,t] \end{bmatrix} = \begin{bmatrix} R_{11} & R_{12} & \dots & R_{1n} \\ R_{21} & R_{22} & \dots & \dots \\ \dots & \dots & \dots & \\ & & R_{ij} & \dots \\ R_{n1} & R_{n2} & \dots & R_{nn} \end{bmatrix} \begin{bmatrix} y[1,t] \\ \dots \\ y[i,t] \\ \dots \\ y[n,t] \end{bmatrix} \qquad \textbf{(5-39)}$$

Note that Equation (5-39) is strictly not algebraic as we just discussed in the last section, but we will use it here and in the following chapters because it captures the physical model accurately. We concentrate on the following Single Factor Risk Authentication Matrix – the *System*. We term it *single factor* because we only considered one risk factor:

$$\boldsymbol{R} = \begin{bmatrix} R_{11} & R_{12} & \dots & R_{1n} \\ R_{21} & R_{22} & \dots & \dots \\ \dots & \dots & \dots & \\ & & R_{ij} & \dots \\ R_{n1} & R_{n2} & \dots & R_{nn} \end{bmatrix} \qquad \textbf{(5-40)}$$

It is perhaps easy to see that all the diagonal terms in Equation (5-39) have the same meaning as in Equation (5-38), i.e. the probability that the modeled risk will strike the corresponding user.

Off diagonal terms also have the same meaning extended to all users. For example, for the *1st* user, we multiply out the first row of Equation (5-39) to get

$$y'[1,t] = R_{11}y[1,t] + R_{12}y[2,t] + \cdots + R_{1i}y[i,t] + \cdots + R_{1n}y[n,t] \quad \textbf{(5-41)}$$

Equation (5-41) is the authentication result (primed quantity) for the first user adjusted for the *specific* risk type that the IAM Systems engineer may have identified and quantified.

The terms of the equation may be interpreted as follows (where we have assumed that the risk matrix in Equation (5-39) models phishing risk):

R_{11} - *The probability or risk that the User 1's login is the subject of a phishing attack.*

R_{12} - *The probability or risk that the User 2's login, being the subject of a phishing attack, makes User 1's login vulnerable to the same risk.*

...

R_{1i} - *The probability or risk that the User i's login, being the subject of a phishing attack, makes User 1's login vulnerable to the same risk.*

...

R_{1n} - *The probability that the last user, User n's account, being the subject of a phishing attack, makes User 1's login vulnerable to the same risk.*

We may rewrite Equation (5-41) for the generic *User l* as:

$$y'[l,t] = \sum_{i=1}^{i=n} R_{li}y[i,t] \tag{5-42}$$

The Authentication Risk Matrix for all users is given in Equation (5-39), with each term having the foregoing meaning and interpretation applied to the corresponding user.

It is easy to show that the above scheme may be extended to more risk types as long as we are careful to come up with a realistic model of the interaction between the risks. We tackle this issue in the next chapter.

SUMMARY

In this chapter, we have modeled the risks attached to an IAM Authentication process. Starting with the generic meaning and implications of trust in human interactions, we proceeded to show that the authentication process modeled in previous chapters may be adjusted for risk by reducing it by a factor equal to the Authentication Risk Matrix.

We then derived this Authentication Risk Matrix in a simplified one risk vector scenario.

In the following chapter, we extend this model to multiple risk vectors (or factors) in order to reach a more complete picture of Authentication System Risk.

Chapter 6 - Trust Models in Identity and Access Management: Modeling Generalized Authentication Risk

INTRODUCTION

In the previous chapter, we arrived at the Single Factor Authentication Risk Matrix:

$$\begin{bmatrix} y'[1,t] \\ \dots \\ y'[i,t] \\ \dots \\ y'[n,t] \end{bmatrix} = \begin{bmatrix} R_{11} & R_{12} & \dots & R_{1n} \\ R_{21} & R_{22} & \dots & \dots \\ \dots & \dots & \dots & \\ & & R_{ij} & \dots \\ R_{n1} & R_{n2} & \dots & R_{nn} \end{bmatrix} \begin{bmatrix} y[1,t] \\ \dots \\ y[i,t] \\ \dots \\ y[n,t] \end{bmatrix} \quad \textbf{(6-1)}$$

Our objective here is to come up with a generalized Risk Matrix that describes all risks associated with all logins and all risks that the IAM Engineer may want to model.

GENERALIZED IAM AUTHENTICATION RISK MATRIX

To come up with a Generalized IAM Authentication Risk Matrix, we will make the same assumptions as before, namely,

- Different risk types strike our users independently of each other. In other words, the risk of any particular user suffering an identity theft attack from a phishing attack vector is independent of that of an attack via a social engineering risk vector, etc.

  Note that we exclude nonidentity-borne threats. For example, a distributed denial of service (DDOS) attack may not depend on any particular identity to cause serious damage to the enterprise. On the other hand, attack vectors may start as nonidentity-borne attacks and evolve into an identity borne one, whereupon the model discussed here may apply to them.

- A single user may suffer multiple types of attack vectors. However, we model the risk that they will be subject to just one of them (*at least one*). This is consistent with the IAM

System being a risk-averse framework – our model should tell us when the user has suffered at least one attack vector. This assumption minimizes the risk to the IAM System by creating a model that is predicated on just one risk vector striking a user. In an IAM System with multiple potential risks, we would like to know the likelihood that just one of the enumerated (modeled) risks has happened. Additionally, it is even more important to base our model on the spread of any single risk since risks that spread can quickly overwhelm the IAM System and put all other identities and organization asset in jeopardy.

- Intuition dictates a multi-risk environment to be riskier even though we cannot know ahead of time how much riskier things will get (probabilities do not add up in general). At any rate, we expect that the generalized risk matrix will have terms that are qualitatively larger than those in the system of Equation (6-1) above.

As before, we start with the simple case of two users (renamed here to User 1 and User 2) and two risk types, a phishing attack (*risk 1, r1*) and a password logger Trojan (*risk 2, r2*).

We enumerate the interesting events as follows:

Event 1: *User 1 suffers a phishing attack, probability* $P(r_{11})$

$$P(Event\ 1) = P(r_{11}) \tag{6-2}$$

Event 2: *User 1 suffers a password logger Trojan attack, probability* $P(r_{21})$

$$P(Event\ 2) = P(r_{21}) \tag{6-3}$$

Event 3: *User 2 suffers a phishing attack, probability* $P(r_{12})$

$$P(Event\ 3) = P(r_{12}) \tag{6-4}$$

Event 4: *User 2 suffers a password logger Trojan attack, probability* $P(r_{22})$

$$P(Event\ 4) = P(r_{22}) \tag{6-5}$$

Event 5: *User 1 suffers a phishing attack and a password logger Trojan attack, probability* $P(r_{11})P(r_{21})$ *(since the two events are independent)*

$$P(Event\ 5) = P(r_{11})P(r_{21}) \tag{6-6}$$

Event 6: *User 2 suffers a phishing attack and a password logger Trojan attack, probability* $P(r_{12})P(r_{22})$ *(since the two events are independent)*

$$P(Event\ 6) = P(r_{12})P(r_{22}) \quad \textbf{(6-7)}$$

***Event 7**: Phishing attack spreads from one user to another, assumed to be independent of the user for simplicity, but may be dependent on risk type, probability* $P(s_1)$

$$P(Event\ 7) = P(s_1) \quad \textbf{(6-8)}$$

***Event 8**: Trojan attack spreads from one user to another, assumed to be independent of the user for simplicity, but may be dependent on risk type, probability* $P(s_2)$

$$P(Event\ 8) = P(s_2) \quad \textbf{(6-9)}$$

Note that in a multi-risk environment, it is actually sometimes more appropriate to think of the following event as well.

> ***Event 8'**: User 1 suffers **at least one** attack, probability* $1 - P(r_{11})P(r_{21})$

$$P(Event\ 8') = 1 - P(Event\ 5) = 1 - P(r_{11})P(r_{21}) \quad \textbf{(6-10)}$$

In the preceding event, Equation (6-10), *we have used the following complementary probability property, defined as*

$$P(\bar{e}) = 1 - P(e) \quad \textbf{(6-11)}$$

where $\bar{e}$ is the complementary of event e.

Our assumptions include parts of ***Event 8'*** *as a lower bound, namely the event when the user suffers exactly one attack.*

Next, we need to calculate the risk of the following set of composite events in order to cater for risk propagation from User 2 to User 1:

Event 9:

{Event 3: *User 2 suffers a phishing attack, probability* $P(r_{12})$

AND

Event 7: *The risk spreads from User 2 to User 1, probability* $P(s_1)\}$.

We may use the following relationship to calculate P(***Event 9***) – similar to Equation (5-20) from Chapter 5:

$$P(A \text{ and } B) = P(A/B)P(B) \quad \textbf{(6-12)}$$

to get:

$$P(Event\ 9) = P(s_1/r_{12})P(r_{12}) \quad \textbf{(6-13)}$$

Similarly, we may define Composite Event 10 as:

Event 10:

*{**Event 4**: User 2 suffers a Trojan logger password attack, probability* $P(r_{22})$

AND

***Event 8:** The risk spreads from User 2 to User 1, probability* $P(s_2)$}.

and

$$P(Event\ 10) = P(s_2/r_{22})P(r_{22}) \quad \textbf{(6-14)}$$

Note:

We consider the event that User 2 suffers both attacks and one of the attacks spreads to User 1 as a degenerative condition in the sense that is already included in Events 9 & 10 by virtue of its independence, or by virtue of it being an included event.

§§

To complete the risk that these two identity-borne threats pose to User 1, we need to consider all the following enumeration of events:

- **Event 1:** *User 1 suffers a phishing attack*

$$P(Event\ 1) = P(r_{11}) \quad \textbf{(6-15)}$$

- **Event 2:** *User 1 suffers a password logger Trojan attack*

$$P(Event\ 2) = P(r_{21}) \quad \textbf{(6-16)}$$

- **Event 9** *(above)*

$$P(Event\ 9) = P(s_1/r_{12})P(r_{12}) \quad \textbf{(6-17)}$$

- **Event 10** *(above)*

$$P(Event\ 10) = P(s_2/r_{22})P(r_{22}) \quad \textbf{(6-18)}$$

User 1, therefore, is at risk if one of these events materializes according to our assumptions above. Using another relationship from basic probability theory

$$\begin{aligned} P(A \text{ or } B \text{ or } C \text{ or } D) \\ &= P(A) + P(B) + P(C) + P(D) \\ &- P(A \text{ and } B) - P(A \text{ and } C) - P(A \text{ and } D) \\ &- P(B \text{ and } C) - P(B \text{ and } D) - P(C \text{ and } D) \\ &+ P(A \text{ and } B \text{ and } C) + P(A \text{ and } B \text{ and } D) \\ &+ P(A \text{ and } C \text{ and } D) + P(B \text{ and } C \text{ and } D) \\ &- P(A \text{ and } B \text{ and } C \text{ and } D) \end{aligned} \quad \textbf{(6-19)}$$

we calculate the risk to User 1 as:

$$\begin{aligned} P(E_1 \text{ or } E_2 \text{ or } E_9 \text{ or } E_{10}) \\ &= P(E_1) + P(E_2) + P(E_9) + P(E_{10}D) \\ &- P(E_1 \text{ and } E_2) - P(E_1 \text{ and } E_9) \\ &- P(E_1 \text{ and } E_{10}) - P(E_2 \text{ and } E_9) \\ &- P(E_2 \text{ and } E_{10}) - P(E_9 \text{ and } E_{10}) \\ &+ P(E_1 \text{ and } E_2 \text{ and } E_9) \\ &+ P(E_1 \text{ and } E_2 \text{ and } E_{10}) \\ &+ P(E_1 \text{ and } E_9 \text{ and } E_{10}) \\ &+ P(E_2 \text{ and } E_9 \text{ and } E_{10}) \\ &- P(E_1 \text{ and } E_2 \text{ and } E_9 \text{ and } E_{10}) \end{aligned} \quad \textbf{(6-20)}$$

or

$$
\begin{aligned}
P(E_1\ or\ E_2\ or\ E_9\ or\ E_{10}) \\
&= P(r_{11}) + P(r_{21}) + P(s_1/r_{12})P(r_{12}) \\
&+ P(s_2/r_{22})P(r_{22}) - P(r_{11})P(r_{21}) \\
&- P(r_{11})P(s_1/r_{12})P(r_{12}) \\
&- P(r_{11})P(s_2/r_{22})P(r_{22}) \\
&- P(r_{21})P(s_1/r_{12})P(r_{12}) \\
&- P(r_{21})P(s_2/r_{22})P(r_{22}) \\
&- P(s_1/r_{12})P(r_{12})P(s_2/r_{22})P(r_{22}) \\
&+ P(r_{11})P(r_{21})P(s_1/r_{12})P(r_{12}) \\
&+ P(r_{11})P(r_{21})P(s_2/r_{22})P(r_{22}) \\
&+ P(r_{11})P(s_1/r_{12})P(r_{12})P(s_2/r_{22})P(r_{22}) \\
&+ P(r_{21})P(s_1/r_{12})P(r_{12})P(s_2/r_{22})P(r_{22}) \\
&- P(r_{11})P(r_{21})P(s_1/r_{12})P(r_{12})P(s_2/r_{22})P(r_{22})
\end{aligned} \qquad \textbf{(6-21)}
$$

In Equation (6-21), we have again used the fact that Event 1 and Event 2 are independent of each other, and so are Event 1 and Event 10, and Event 9 and Event 10, etc., such that their individual probabilities may be multiplied to calculate their joint probabilities. Joint probability in this case is the chance of all the enumerated events materializing at once.

We simplify Equation (6-21) by identifying the following terms:

$$\beta_1 = P(s_1/r_{12}) \qquad \textbf{(6-22)}$$

and

$$\beta_2 = P(s_2/r_{22}) \qquad \textbf{(6-23)}$$

As we may recall from Event 9, $P(s_1/r_{12})$ is the risk that a phishing attack will spread from User 2 given that User 2 is attacked, and similarly for a Trojan attack.

We define this property of the risk as its ***'beta'***, and it is a measure of the property of the risk to spread from one user to another within the enterprise:

Identity-Borne Risk Beta, β:

A measure of an identity-borne risk to spread from one identity to another.

β is the risk propagation 'beta', a measure of the propensity of the risk to spread from one user to another within a particular enterprise – in this case from User 2 to User 1.

The best illustration of Identity-Borne Risk Beta is perhaps from the worm class of viruses that infect user computers. If the dispersion vector is via a user's email contacts list, the beta may be relatively high compared to say a phishing attack that targets an infrequently used enterprise application.

By way of another example, an engineered Trojan may have a high β (since a high beta maximizes its malicious actor creator's profits), while a workstation session hijack may have a relatively low β, perhaps because the latter may require a user to log in before it can hijack the session.

§§

Using the individual risk beta, we may rewrite Equation (6-21)as follows

$$\begin{aligned} P(User\ 1\ is\ Attacked) \\ &= P(r_{11}) + P(r_{21}) + \beta_1 P(r_{12}) + \beta_2 P(r_{22}) \\ &- P(r_{11})P(r_{21}) - \beta_1 P(r_{11})P(r_{12}) \\ &- \beta_2 P(r_{11})P(r_{22}) - \beta_1 P(r_{21})P(r_{12}) \\ &- \beta_2 P(r_{21})P(r_{22}) - \beta_1\beta_2 P(r_{12})P(r_{22}) \\ &+ \beta_1 P(r_{11})P(r_{21})P(r_{12}) \\ &+ \beta_2 P(r_{11})P(r_{21})P(r_{22}) \\ &+ \beta_1\beta_2 P(r_{11})P(r_{12})P(r_{22}) \\ &+ \beta_1\beta_2 P(r_{21})P(r_{12})P(r_{22}) \\ &- \beta_1\beta_2 P(r_{11})P(r_{21})P(r_{12})P(r_{22}) \end{aligned} \quad \textbf{(6-24)}$$

As before, we may estimate User 1's risk adjusted authentication result by dropping the mixed terms that have 3 or more multiplicands in Equation (6-24), noting that the second index denotes the user, to get

$$y'[1,t] \approx [P(r_{11}) + P(r_{21}) - P(r_{11})P(r_{21})]y[1,t] + [\beta_1 P(r_{12}) + \beta_2 P(r_{22})]y[2,t] \quad \textbf{(6-25)}$$

In Equation (6-25), we have once again relaxed strict algebraic correspondence in the sense of Equation (5-38), Chapter 5.

Similarly,

$$
\begin{aligned}
&P(User\ 2\ is\ Attacked) \\
&\quad = P(r_{12}) + P(r_{22}) + \beta_1 P(r_{11}) + \beta_2 P(r_{21}) \\
&\quad - P(r_{12})P(r_{22}) - \beta_1 P(r_{12})P(r_{11}) \\
&\quad - \beta_2 P(r_{12})P(r_{21}) - \beta_1 P(r_{22})P(r_{11}) \\
&\quad - \beta_2 P(r_{22})P(r_{21}) - \beta_1\beta_2 P(r_{11})P(r_{21}) \\
&\quad + \beta_1 P(r_{12})P(r_{22})P(r_{11}) \\
&\quad + \beta_2 P(r_{12})P(r_{22})P(r_{21}) + \beta_1\beta_2 P(r_{12})P(r_{21}) \\
&\quad + \beta_1\beta_2 P(r_{22})P(r_{11})P(r_{21}) \\
&\quad - \beta_1\beta_2 P(r_{12})P(r_{22})P(r_{11})P(r_{21})
\end{aligned}
\qquad \textbf{(6-26)}
$$

and

$$y'[2,t] \approx [P(r_{12}) + P(r_{22}) - P(r_{12})P(r_{22})]y[2,t] + [\beta_1 P(r_{11}) + \beta_2 P(r_{21})]y[1,t] \qquad \textbf{(6-27)}$$

Our 2x2-Factor (2 users, 2 risk types) Authentication Risk Matrix then becomes, following preceding approximations:

$$\begin{bmatrix} y'[1,t] \\ y'[2,t] \end{bmatrix} = \begin{bmatrix} P(r_{11}) + P(r_{21}) - P(r_{11})P(r_{21}) & \beta_1 P(r_{12}) + \beta_2 P(r_{22}) \\ \beta_1 P(r_{11}) + \beta_2 P(r_{21}) & P(r_{12}) + P(r_{22}) - P(r_{12})P(r_{22}) \end{bmatrix} \begin{bmatrix} y[A,t] \\ y[B,t] \end{bmatrix} \qquad \textbf{(6-28)}$$

We may expand the 2-factor Authentication Risk Matrix to *n*-users and *k*-risk types by noticing the diagonal symmetry of Equation (6-28), thus:

$$\begin{bmatrix} y'[1,t] \\ \dots \\ y'[i,t] \\ \dots \\ y'[n,t] \end{bmatrix} = \begin{bmatrix} R_{11} & R_{12} & \dots & R_{1n} \\ R_{21} & R_{22} & \dots & \dots \\ \dots & \dots & \dots & \\ & & R_{ij} & \dots \\ R_{n1} & R_{n2} & \dots & R_{nn} \end{bmatrix} \begin{bmatrix} y[1,t] \\ \dots \\ y[i,t] \\ \dots \\ y[n,t] \end{bmatrix} \quad \textbf{(6-29)}$$

where now,

$R_{ij}\big|_{i=j}$ are diagonal components that indicate the probability that the User *j* suffers the *i*[th] of *k* identity-borne attacks, with probability $R_{ij} = P(r_{ij})$

and

$R_{ij}\big|_{i\neq j}$, the off-diagonal terms, indicate the probability that User *j*, having suffered an attack of one risk type out of possible *k* risk types, transfers it to 'diagonal' user,

$P(s_i)$ is the probability that risk *i* will spread from one user to another (independent of the user)

and finally,

β_i is the enterprise risk propagation beta for risk type *i*, i.e. the conditional probability of that identity borne risk spreading.

It is also perhaps easy to see that the diagonal terms in Equation (6-29), for any user *j*, are of the form:

$$R_{jj} = \sum_{i=1}^{i=k} \left(P(r_{ij}) + smaller\ terms \right) \qquad \textbf{(6-30)}$$

The smaller terms are multiplicative fractions (i.e. unlikely events signified by joint probabilities) of the same order as the sums and may be ignored, thus,

$$R_{jj} \approx \sum_{i=1}^{i=k} P(r_{ij}) \qquad \textbf{(6-31)}$$

The off-diagonal terms may be given by the expression:

$$R_{ij} \approx \sum_{j=1}^{j=n} \left(\sum_{i=1, i \neq j}^{i=k} \beta_i \, P(r_{ij}) \right) \qquad \textbf{(6-32)}$$

Even with our approximations, it is starkly clear that a multi-risk authentication matrix above is far riskier than the single or 2-factor authentication risk matrices discussed above.

BACK (AND FORWARD) PROPAGATING THE AUTHENTICATION RISK MATRIX

The risk matrix derived in Equation (6-29) is a little bit disconcerting because it is applied to the end result of the authentication. In Identity and Access Management (as indeed in other risk mitigation systems) it is more natural to model risk at the entry points since this allows us to separate internal vs. external risks. Internal risks may still be modeled separately, but the segregation allows the IAM systems engineer to take into account the different characteristics of internal vs. external risks and apply appropriate mitigation actions and controls.

We may represent the logical view of the authentication system with respect to risk model entry points as follows:

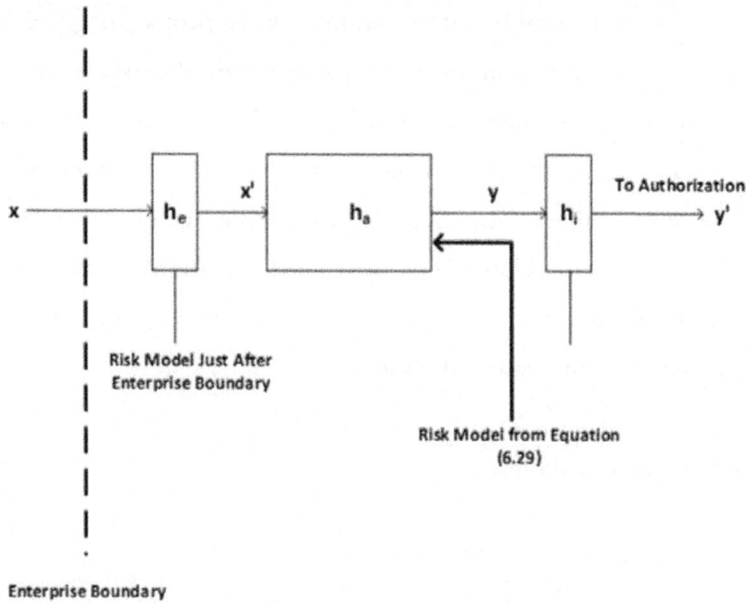

Figure 6-1: Risk Back Propagation Across IAM Systems

In Figure 6-1 and in Equation (6-29), it is important to understand that y' represents *all preceding accumulated risks* up to the point the credentials exit the Authentication System, h_a. In other words, our risks assumptions should include all intervening systems, processes and all their pertaining characteristics.

It therefore follows that we may propagate the results from Post-Authentication to the enterprise boundary by simply changing our model of the risks associated with Equation (6-29) to apply to credentials entering the enterprise. We have to change our definition of risk propagation beta, β_i , to apply to external credentials, but otherwise there is no analytical difficulty in carrying out the back propagation.

We may, however, still be interested in forward propagating a risk matrix through another component or system within the organization or enterprise. This may happen, for example, if a middleware system is used to interface with applications. This could also be done in a relatively simple conceptual manner. For example, we may consider a session management scheme as a post-authentication system with risks separate and distinct from those of the authentication system and that requires a different risk model.

We may proceed as follows.

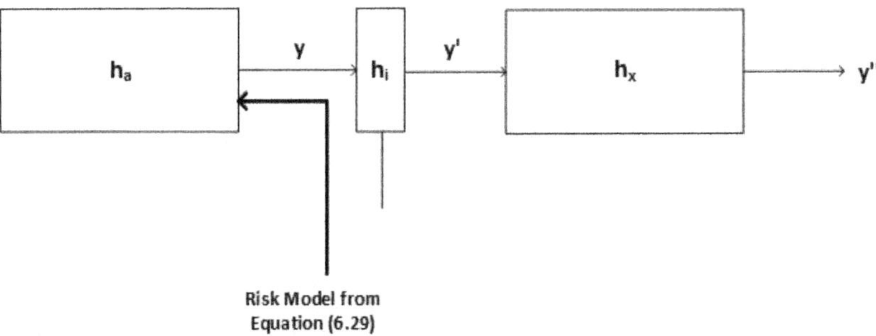

Figure 6-2: IAM Risk Propagation

Because of the analysis in the previous section, we know that regardless of the risk of the unknown system (denoted in Figure 6-2 by h_x), it must result in the risk-adjusted output, y'', being on the form,

$$y'' = h_x y' \qquad \textbf{(6-33)}$$

because

$$y' = Ry \tag{6-34}$$

it follows immediately that

$$y'' = h_x y' = h_x R y \tag{6-35}$$

i.e. the risk matrices multiply as we move across our enterprise, a result which is somewhat surprising, simple and elegant.

We may validate this result by considering a simple and limiting case whereby all the off-diagonal terms in Equation (6-29) vanish, and we then have, from Equation (6-35):

$$y'' = I_h I_R y \tag{6-36}$$

where I_h and I_R are diagonal matrices representing the two modeled risk regimes above. Since both systems are diagonal, each term in Equation (6-36) is of the form

$$y''[i,t] = h_{ij} R_{ij} y[i,t] \tag{6-37}$$

If we consider cascading risks in Equation (6-37) as independently occurring, then their probabilities multiply and Equation (6-37) is a statement regarding the likelihood of two independent risks occurring to the same user if we keep in mind that our model of risk, represented by R_{ij} and h_{ij}, is predicated on the user suffering one of *k* independent risk vectors.

Interpretation of Authentication Risk

It may be instructive to try to understand and interpret what the introduction of risk does to our user credentials model.

As you may recall from Chapter 3, we represented our credentials as a unit sample function:

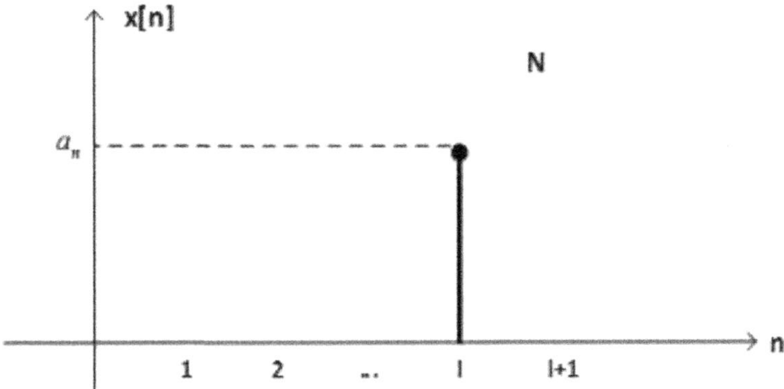

Figure 6-3: User Credential Representation

When we introduce risk, the overall effect is that the credential is no longer a well-defined quantity having a specific height, a_n and located precisely at some index l relative to the credentials store. Instead, the real credentials will have some height which is slightly less than a_n, and will have some distribution (or spread in 'identity energy') around the location where we think it is (or should be!). We depict this interpretation below:

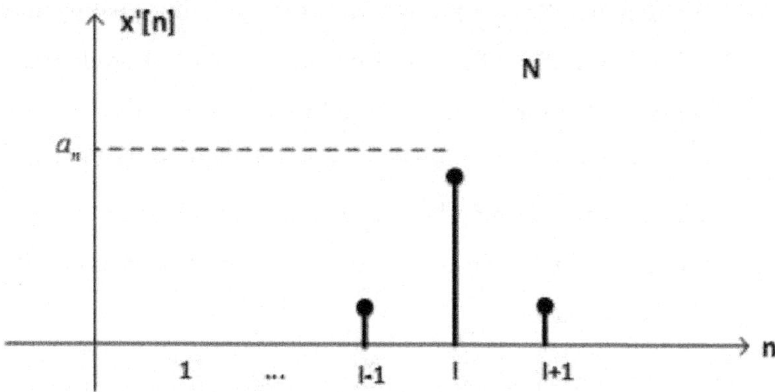

Figure 6-4: Risk Adjusted Credentials (Unit Sample Representation)

Note that our authentication result from Chapter 2, Equation (2-22), also needs to be modified:

$$y[n] = \sum_{m=0}^{m=n} \vec{a}_l * \vec{b}_n * \delta[l-m] * \delta[m] \tag{6-38}$$

- First of all, we have to model some uncertainty into stored credentials – i.e. even the 'correct' credentials will be spread around some mean location according to the results of this section. As a consequence, this model allows for a scenario whereby the correct credentials are not stored where we expect them to be, but in an entirely different location (resulting in a user supplying the correct credentials and yet getting denied access by virtue of non-authentication). Even as the model contemplates it, the possibility of this occurring is close to zero.

- We may need to drop our strict orthogonality assumption above, and allow for the 'bleeding' of stored credentials across the dimensions – we don't consider this scenario in our treatment below, but note that it is a valid adjustment that may be made to accommodate risk even though its inclusion or otherwise does not fundamentally alter our model.

- The credentials representation of Figure 6-4 is one dimensional, i.e. all its components are assumed to be contained entirely in one of the dimensions of an N-dimensional orthogonal space. Once again, we may relax this assumption without much difficulty.

With the above assumptions, some readers may recognize that the resulting authentication (or convolution) result will have the form depicted below, with 'identity energies' spread symmetrically around the presumed correct stored credentials location. This should be compared to Figure 2-11, Chapter 2.

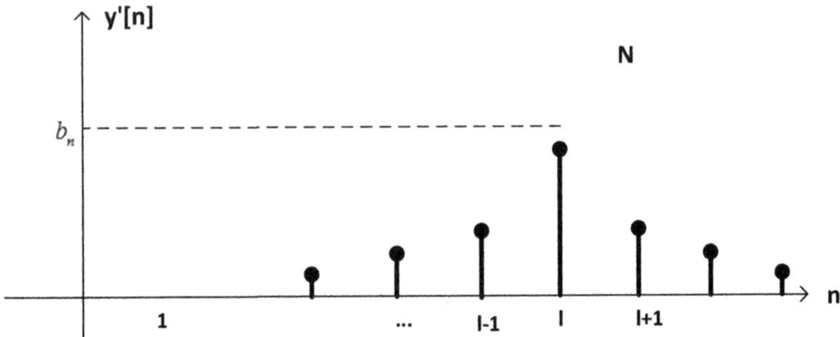

Figure 6-5: Representation of Risk Adjusted Authentication Result

SUMMARY

In this chapter, we have extended the authentication risk model from the previous chapter to an enterprise that contains multiple users and multiple risks, i.e. a real life scenario that depicts an enterprise that is faced with multiple risk vectors. We started with a simple scenario of two users and two risk vectors, and with only a few assumptions extended the simple result to include all users and an arbitrary number of risk types.

We have also provided the reader with a framework of evolving the risk model from one entry point within the enterprise to another. Specifically, we found that Risk Systems exhibit a multiplicative property from one entry point to another, allowing for a consistent systems approach to be applied at multiple individual points then combined into an enterprise wide risk profile.

Lastly we have provided the reader with a systems interpretation of risk, and re-cast some of our prior results into risk adjusted models.

In the next chapter we will deal with several models that may be applied to authorization risks.

Chapter 7 - Trust Models in Identity and Access Management: Modeling Authorization Risk

INTRODUCTION

In this chapter, we will analyze risk as it applies to the IAM Authorization System. We use the results of Chapter 3, which modeled IAM Authorization as a matrix of assertions, as the starting point and include risk in that model.

First, we divide IAM Authorization risk into two types, Possessor-in-Fraud risk and Fraud-in-Possessor risk. We show that Possessor-in-Fraud authorization risk may be modeled simply by assigning an uncertainty to the user authentication risk matrix, but that the Fraud-in-Possessor risk is somewhat more complicated, involving some time-dependent modeling.

In either case, we show that the two risk types may be evolved (propagated) from one enterprise sub-system (or end-point) to another using a derived probabilistic (Bayesian) model.

RISK IN AUTHORIZATION

In Chapter 3, we derived the IAM Authorization System. The derived equation was recast in Equation (5-3), Chapter 5 as given below:

$$A(x_l, t) = \begin{bmatrix} t_1r_1 & t_1r_2 & \cdots & t_1r_n \\ t_2r_1 & t_2r_2 & \cdots & \cdots \\ \cdots & \cdots & \cdots & \\ & & t_ir_j & \cdots \\ t_mr_1 & t_mr_1 & \cdots & t_mr_n \end{bmatrix} \begin{bmatrix} 1 & 0 & \cdots & 0 \\ 0 & 1 & \cdots & \cdots \\ \cdots & \cdots & \cdots & \\ & & 1 & \cdots \\ 0 & 0 & \cdots & 1 \end{bmatrix} x_i \qquad \textbf{(7-1)}$$

Where A_{ij} is the assertion for the resource r_i based on the role t_j, and x_l is the user identity.

We may think of the assertions in Equation (7-1) as propagating across the enterprise applications as depicted in Figure 5-2, Chapter 5 above (reproduced below)

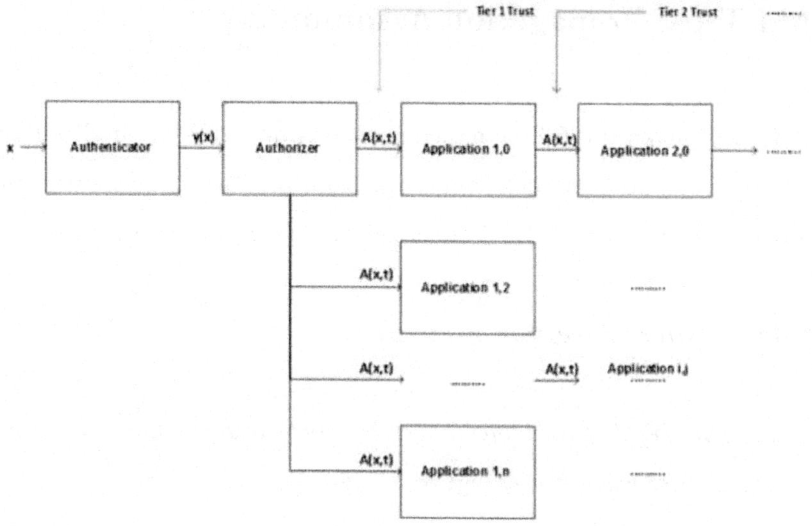

Figure 7-1: IAM Trust Propagation (Same as Figure 5-2 , Chapter 5)

The question of this chapter then becomes:

> *How do we model the risks tied to this propagation?*
>
> *Furthermore, as the assertions are generated from multiple enterprise systems, how do we account for any risks that may come from these other systems?*

We tackle these questions next.

IAM Trust Propagation Assumptions

We will make the following assumptions in order to simplify our Authorization Risk model. These assumptions are consistent with how organizations may use Authorization Assertions in practice.

Assumption: Assertion Propagation

Assertions may be passed from the Authorizer to an application or from one application to another. (See Figure 7-1 *above)*

Assumption: Assertion Validation

Applications may or may not verify the validity of the assertions with the Authorizer. If the application chooses not to verify the validity of the assertions, it must trust that the upstream application did not modify it, benignly or maliciously.

Note:
We are less concerned with the details of assertion validation, and put all types of assertion validation at par for the purposes of our model. For example, a digital signature validation would be equivalent to a service-based validation in our model.

Assumption: Possessor Intentions

> *The model we derive below is intention-agnostic since we cannot know an actor's intentions ahead of time. Thus the correct assertions in the wrong hands or the wrong assertions in benign hands each portends risk to the IAM system even though their consequences may turn out to be quite different materially. The malicious assertions holder may use them to injure the firm or organization, while the benign holder of incorrectly assigned assertions may report the error and have it corrected.*

With these assumptions, we may think of two types of IAM Authorization risks, namely *Possessor-in-Fraud* risk – whereby valid assertions are held by a fraudulent identity – and *Fraud-in-Possessor* risk whereby invalid assertions are held by a valid identity.

Note that per assumptions above, the latter case includes the scenarios whereby a valid identity benignly holds invalid assertions due to errors not of their active commission. However, refer to Chapter 4 on models to resolve or minimize Fraud-in-Possessor type errors.

Modeling IAM Authorization Possessor-in-Fraud Risk

An IAM Possessor-in-Fraud risk involves a malicious actor replaying assertions that were obtained from a legitimate user. Possessor-in-Fraud risk also occurs when the malicious actor obtains valid credentials and uses them to impersonate a valid user and thereby obtains their assertions fraudulently.

In Equation (6-29) of Chapter 6, we modeled the authentication risk for all users using the Authentication Risk Matrix, thus:

$$\begin{bmatrix} y'[1,t] \\ \cdots \\ y'[i,t] \\ \cdots \\ y'[n,t] \end{bmatrix} = \begin{bmatrix} R_{11} & R_{12} & \cdots & R_{1n} \\ R_{21} & R_{22} & \cdots & \cdots \\ \cdots & \cdots & \cdots & \\ & & R_{ij} & \cdots \\ R_{n1} & R_{n2} & \cdots & R_{nn} \end{bmatrix} \begin{bmatrix} y[1,t] \\ \cdots \\ y[i,t] \\ \cdots \\ y[n,t] \end{bmatrix} \qquad \textbf{(7-2)}$$

From the above equation, we see that the risk of type Possessor-in-Fraud is simply the associated authentication risk multiplied by the appropriate column of the Authentication Risk Matrix.

In Chapter 5, the IAM Authorization System was derived, Equation (7-1) above.

We can combine Equations (7-1) and (7-2) in a straightforward manner as follows.

For the user x_l, the risk-adjusted authentication is given by one of the vector elements of Equation (7-2), i.e.:

$$y'[l,t] = \sum_{i=1}^{i=n} R_{il} y[i,t] \qquad \textbf{(7-3)}$$

If we recall the model expression for authentication result from Chapter 2,

$$y[n] = \vec{h}_a[n] * \vec{x}_i[n] \qquad \textbf{(7-4)}$$

it follows by simple substitution, after re-indexing and adding time dependence, that

$$y'[l,t] = \sum_{i=1}^{i=n} R_{il} \vec{h}_a[l,t] * \bar{x}[l,t] \qquad \textbf{(7-5)}$$

In Equation (7-5), we have dropped the subscript in favor of argument notation, and added time dependence.

Substituting Equation (7-5) into Equation (7-1) above, noting that $y'[l,t]$ is the risk adjusted User Identity x_l post authentication, we derive the risk adjusted Assertion Matrix for the Possessor-in-Fraud case as follows.

$$A(x_l,t) = \left(\sum_{i=1}^{i=n} R_{il}\right)\begin{bmatrix} t_1r_1 & t_1r_2 & \dots & t_1r_n \\ t_2r_1 & t_2r_2 & \dots & \dots \\ \dots & \dots & \dots & \\ & & t_ir_j & \dots \\ t_mr_1 & t_mr_1 & \dots & t_mr_n \end{bmatrix}\begin{bmatrix} 1 & 0 & \dots & 0 \\ 0 & 1 & \dots & \dots \\ \dots & \dots & \dots & \\ & & 1 & \dots \\ 0 & 0 & \dots & 1 \end{bmatrix}\left(\vec{h}_a[l,t] * \bar{x}[l,t]\right) \qquad \textbf{(7-6)}$$

In Equation (7-6), we realize that the reduction term from Equation (7-3) is really a scalar quantity once the summation over all users is carried out (to take into account Authentication Risk propagation model described in Chapter 6).

It is also necessary that we preserve the operator implied by Equation (7-1) above. It also behooves us to ensure that the roles operator is executed before the convolution for the user authentication is completed.

In other words, Equation (7-6) simply takes each assertion and reduces its certainty uniformly by the authentication uncertainty of their possessor. *This is intuitively correct because we may not assign to any assertions a higher level of credibility than their possessor's authenticity.*

§§

The curious reader may note from the previous Chapter that with the introduction of risk to the authentication and authorization system models, the user identity is never a settled matter – i.e. there always exists some doubt about the user's identity. In this sense, Equation (7-3) is always true even when we are modeling the Possessor-in-Fraud as above, or Fraud-in-Possessor (see below section).

To remove this analytical and logical difficulty, we may simply leave the Possessor-in-Fraud model above in the following Fraud-in-Possessor treatment. However, in practice, separating the two (and assuming the possessor-in-fraud risk is non-existent in cases of fraud-in-possessor) provides a more practical framework for managing organizational risk by segregating the authorization threats by type. Furthermore, it is sometimes not in practical doubt what the possessor's identity is, for example, when the user is presenting their multi-factor credentials in person.

Modeling IAM Authorization Fraud-in-Possessor Risk

A Fraud-in-Possessor risk manifests because a legitimate identity holds assertions that may not reflect his true entitlement. By "true entitlement", we mean those that were intended by the legitimate controlling organizational authority – i.e. we consider both non-malicious process and technical mistakes in the entitlement issuance process as exhibiting Fraud-in-Possessor risk to the enterprise.

In many ways, Fraud-in-Possessor risks are much more challenging to model than their Possessor-in-Fraud counterparts. This is because a user's authorization is built from multiple sources, with each source potentially introducing multiple independent (or even worse, dependent) risks. The IAM System that builds up the user's assertions, therefore, needs to keep in mind that each element of the assertion in Equation 3.25 is at best uncertain.

We may proceed by analyzing the risks inherent in each system that produces the assertion elements:

$$User\ Assertions = A = \begin{bmatrix} t_1 r_1 & t_1 r_2 & \dots & t_1 r_n \\ t_2 r_1 & t_2 r_2 & \dots & \dots \\ \dots & \dots & \dots & \\ & & t_i r_j & \dots \\ t_m r_1 & t_m r_1 & \dots & t_m r_n \end{bmatrix} \quad \textbf{(7-7)}$$

If we assume that each assertion source system is characterized in terms of its risk (and it is safe to assume each source or group of sources, will have different risk characteristics depending on "intrinsic" technical, process, and other factors), we may then reduce each term in Equation (7-7) by the corresponding and properly modeled uncertainty term.

As you may recall from Chapter 3, each term of the Authorization Matrix (Equation 6.3) represents a different operation on the user. In an enterprise setting, such an operation on the user carries risk and uncertainty. For example, the user attribute on which such an operation depends may have been stored incorrectly (data integrity issues). Even more ominously, the store on which the calculation depends may be compromised by a malicious actor. The resulting Risk Adjusted User Assertions, A', may then be described as follows, using the same interpretation of risk as before:

$$A' = \begin{bmatrix} R_{11}t_1r_1 & R_{12}t_1r_2 & \dots & R_{1n}t_1r_n \\ R_{21}t_2r_1 & R_{22}t_2r_2 & \dots & \dots \\ \dots & \dots & \dots & \\ & & R_{ij}t_ir_j & \dots \\ R_{m1}t_mr_1 & R_{m2}t_mr_1 & \dots & R_{mn}t_mr_n \end{bmatrix} \quad \textbf{(7-8)}$$

In Equation (7-8) R_{ij} is the uncertainty associated with calculating assertion A_{ij} for the user.

FRAUD-IN-POSSESSOR RISK DERIVATION AND PROPAGATION

Introduction

Whether the user's assertions manifests Possessor-in-Fraud or Fraud-in-Possessor, we expect that the enterprise will face the greatest threat from risks that spread from one user to another.

In this section, we will model the derivation of fraud-in-possessor risk. Additionally, we look at a model of how such risks evolve.

To aid the following treatment, we will start by expanding the definition of the user's assertion to include

All tokens that the user presents to gain access to restricted organizational resources.

Using this expanded definition, we may include, for example, the assigned picture badge/id that the user swipes at the front door or the electronic token she uses to sign-on to her computer or application.

Analytically, the form stays the same as before (Equation (3-39), Chapter 3) since we did not assume in that Chapter that the assertions had to take any form or be derived/calculated using any specific manner. In other words, we combine physical and electronic assertions to get the complete Authorization Matrix for the user.

Second, we will assume, without proof, that at any point we may separate the risk terms in the Risk Adjusted Assertions Matrix, Equation (7-8), and write it using Equation (7-7) as follows:

$$\bar{A'} = \bar{R} * \bar{A} \qquad \textbf{(7-9)}$$

where $\bar{R}$ is a risk matrix that transforms the non-risk adjusted Assertion Matrix, $\bar{A}$, to its risk adjusted version, $\bar{A'}$. In theory, there is no reason why the decomposition in Equation (7-9) *should not be* possible.

With these assumptions, we may posit as follows:

Proposition I:

The Fraud-in-Possessor Risk Matrix $\bar{R}$ *is time dependent.*

In other words, contrary to perception, a user's assertions will change over time since, while the (nominal) assertions themselves may not be time dependent, the risk profile is time dependent because the Fraud-in-Possessor Risk System $\bar{R}$ changes over time. We have excluded any explicit time dependence in the assertions like time access restrictions, session limits, expirations and other explicit time-variable impositions that organizational policy may attach to an assertion.

Proposition II:

The Fraud-in-Possessor Risk Matrix contains two components: one component is deterministic in the sense that we can probabilistically predict or calculate what its value is going to be while the other value is entirely random.

The Fraud-in-Possessor Risk Matrix is thus a system of time-dependent random variables:

$$\bar{A}'(t) = \bar{R}(t) * \bar{A} \tag{7-10}$$

In the next sections, we provide a sketch of a framework for understanding the nature of this time-dependent random system that represents the fundamental risk associated with the IAM Authorization.

Note:

The following treatment consciously avoids mathematically difficult formulation in favor of a more easily accessible one using basic probability theory concepts. The astute reader may discern that we have treated risk posed to the fraud-in-possessor authorization process as a stochastic process in finite time. We believe our treatment captures the fundamental nature of the stochastic process without the mathematical difficulty that a full blown stochastic analysis would entail.

Derivation

In deriving the probability of risk tied to a particular authorization source, i.e. each team of the Risk Matrix $\bar{R}(t)$ in Equation (7-10), there are several methods we may use.

We may decide to go with an empirical actuarial approach based on past data. We may also follow a process-based approach where each risk factor is modeled to arrive at the authorization source risk. We may also use ITPM (based on Capital Markets approach). The interested reader may find these and plenty others in the literature, for example, (Orondo, 2008) or (Mukhopadhyay, 2008).

Our goal here, however, is to convey fundamental ideas that underlie most if not all of these models, rather than prescribe a particular approach.

The fundamental problem is to find risk associated with each element of our Authorization Risk Matrix. Each such risk is ultimately tied to the corresponding authorization source according to Equation (7-8).

If we knew the risk of each authorization source, we would simply reduce the Authorization matrix accordingly, as we already saw before:

$$User\ Assertions = A(x_l,t) = \begin{bmatrix} R_{11}t_1r_1 & R_{12}t_1r_2 \\ R_{21}t_2r_1 & R_{22}t_2r_2 \end{bmatrix} \begin{bmatrix} 1 & 0 \\ 0 & 1 \end{bmatrix} x_l \quad \textbf{(7-11)}$$

In Equation (7-11), we have simplified the risk adjusted generic authorization matrix to a simple 2 resource, 2 role organization.

Assuming the user, per organization policy, possesses *role 1* but not *role 2*, and *role 1* is assigned to *resource 1*, and *role 2* is assigned to *resource 2*, then, per the results from Chapter 3, Equation (3-47):

$$t_1(r_1x_l) = r_1t_1x_l + x_lt_1r_1 = 0.5 + 0.5 = 1 \quad \textbf{(7-12)}$$

$$t_1(r_2x_l) = r_2t_1x_l + x_lt_1r_2 = 0 + 0.5 = 0.5 \quad \textbf{(7-13)}$$

$$t_2(r_1x_l) = r_1t_2x_l + x_lt_2r_1 = 0 + 0 = 0 \quad \textbf{(7-14)}$$

$$t_2(r_2x_l) = r_2t_2x_l + x_lt_2r_2 = 0.5 + 0 = 0.5 \quad \textbf{(7-15)}$$

Using the same 0.75 quantum as in Chapter 3, Equation (7-11) becomes

$$User\ Assertions = A(x_l,t) = \begin{bmatrix} R_{11} & 0 \\ 0 & 0 \end{bmatrix} \begin{bmatrix} 1 & 0 \\ 0 & 1 \end{bmatrix} x_l \quad \textbf{(7-16)}$$

If the authorization risk matrix were known, we could simply substitute it into Equation (7-16) to get the User Assertions.

Actually, if R_{11} *is a measure of risk in the preceding sense, i.e. the probability that the user does not have the corresponding role that they are holding, it may be more appropriate to use the complementary probability in Equation* (7-16), $(1 - R_{11})$, *etc. In this case, we may interpret each term as a measure of the confidence level associated with the Assertion. Confidence in this case is the opposite of risk.*

Obviously, we do not know ahead of time what the risk associated with an authorization source is. Besides we are often more concerned with what the risk is going to be in the future.

To calculate the future risk profile of an authentication source, one way to go about it is to start by looking into the past.

Looking into the past, we may define all events that constitute a breach on the authentication source that have occurred in the past. These may include past occurrences of virus attacks, Trojan attacks, software defects, etc., all that work together to make any assertion that comes from that source to be in doubt.

Using all these events we build and *test* a *hypothesis* of what the *future risk* of that authorization source is likely to be. For our purposes, this is the probability that the assertion derived from that authentication source is not authentic.

Thus, suppose upon analyzing our past data, and employing the talents of IAM engineers and statisticians, we decide that the authorization risk of a particular source is $P(H)$, i.e. this is our hypothesis about the risk of the authorization source, and may simply be the previously observed risk associated with the source (this is the *prior* probability):

$$P(H) = Prior\ Probability \tag{7-17}$$

We can them simply wait for (or actively look for) an interesting (and unfortunate) event or a series of events to visit that source (noting that the event need not happen within the organization; it may be external – for example, a new vulnerability affecting the authentication source of system may be discovered). Or nothing at all may happen, even though this would be rare in a dynamic interconnected environment like the Internet.

Note:

We call the prior probability a hypothesis since the past does not predict the future in a probabilistic (stochastic) system. So even though $P(H)$ is the past probability of risk associated with the authorization source, it is not taken as a given, but rather as a starting point or hypothesis.

Let's call the probability of our new observation $P(D)$. Note that $P(D)$ is also *a priori* probability, and must be non-zero according to our definition above i.e., we wait for or actively look for interesting events affecting the authorization source to occur.

$$P(D(T = t)) = The\ Probability\ of\ a\ New\ Observation\ at\ time\ t \tag{7-18}$$

According to Bayes Theorem (named for the 18th Century English Presbyterian minister and Mathematician Thomas Bayes, 1702 – 1761) in Probability Theory, we can calculate the *probability* that our hypothesis is true using the following formula:

$$P(H/D(t)) = \frac{P(D(t)/H)P(H)}{P(D(t))} \tag{7-19}$$

where

$P(H/D)$ is the conditional probability that the hypothesis is true given the new information and prior data. Note that $P(H/D)$ is a forward looking quantity, and may be considered to be providing a correction of the past information using new information. Lastly, note that $P(H/D)$ is equivalent to the *updated* probability of risk associated with our authentication source in our formulation, and is also a statement about the *probability* that our prior *belief about that authorization source* is correct.

and

$P(D/H)$ is the conditional probability of observing the new information about the authentication source given our hypothesis. In other words, if our hypothesis were correct, $P(D/H)$ is the probability of the new observation happening.

We understand Equation (7-19) as continuously updating our view of authorization risk by combining past data and beliefs with new information in a theoretically sound manner. Equation (7-19) lies at the foundation of many methods of understanding and calculation risk in systems such as ours.

We illustrate this in the following pictorial.

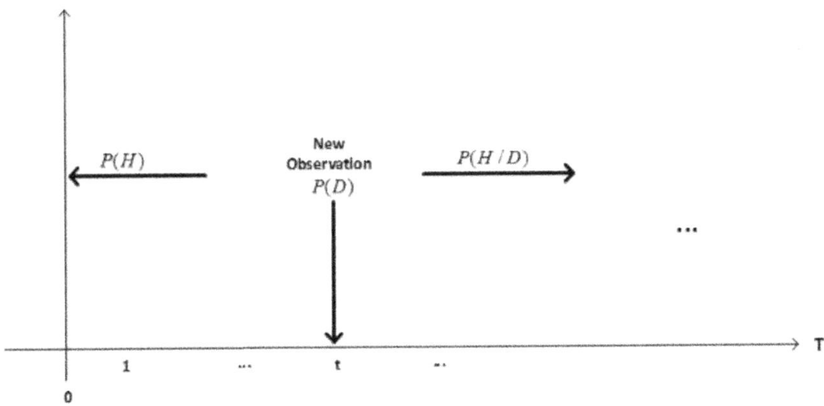

Figure 7-2: Illustrated Bayes Theorem as applied to Authorization Source Risk Model

In Figure 7-2 we have used time as the dependent variable. An interesting event or observation for the authorization source occurs randomly at time $T = t$ with probability $P(D)$. Using this new information, we update our prior estimate or hypothesis or belief about the risk of the authentication source from $P(H)$ to $P(H/D)$.

Applying Bayes Theorem to our prior example, Equation (7-16), we get, using primed quantities to denote updated probabilities:

$$R_{11} = \frac{P(D/R_{11})R_{11}}{P(D)} \tag{7-20}$$

$$R_{11} = R_{21} = R_{22} = 0 \qquad \textbf{(7-21)}$$

where we have assumed, as before, that $P(D)$ does not vanish.

One may ask how we derive the value of R_{11} *in the first place so we can use it in Equation* (7-20). *As it turns out, the initial value of* R_{11} *is not critically important to the Bayes Inference Machine (as the prior set of equations are sometimes referred to) even though care should be taken to choose a reasonable value. Once this is done, the equations are self-correcting based on observed events. In other words, Equations* (7-20)-(7-21) *telescope or converge to the correct value of the underlying probabilities as we recursively update the prior probabilities using new and past observed data.*

Randomness Factor

The derivation in prior section yields the *a posteriori* probability associated with an authorization source risk. We have assumed that the new observed events occur randomly, but once they occur, we can estimate fairly accurately their nominal probabilities and employ Bayes' Theorem to estimate the forward looking probabilities.

To conclude this section, therefore, and in accordance with *Proposition II* above, we will model a random element into each observation. The randomness is assumed to originate from our inability, given observed data affecting the authorization source, to predict the effect of the risk on any given user's assertions. The randomness could also be simply fundamental to the process akin to Heisenberg's Uncertainty Principle in Quantum physics which states that there is an irreducible quantity of randomness in nature.

We give some examples below:

I. *A software vulnerability affecting an authorization source may require the user to execute specific sequence of steps before their assertions are affected by the vulnerability. Moreover, the sequence of steps may not necessarily be preventable via user education or any other preventive actions that the organization may take.*

II. *It may simply be impossible, within reasonable time and within present computing constraints, to analyze the effects of an interesting event on an authorization (or authentication) source.*

III. *There may simply be a fundamental constraint, that, even with completely characterized observed events, the effects on the authorization source and hence the user assertion, will still be so un-predictable as to appear completely random. This may be due to the many un-predictable factors involved: internal and external actors, internal and external organizational processes, etc.*

IV. *Predicting computer program behavior is a fundamental problem in computer science. In other words, at present time, it is impossible to predict how computer code will behave for all possible program inputs, even if such program were to follow the Confinement Problem discussed earlier.*

Taking this randomness factor into consideration, we may complete our model of the authorization risk matrix by adding a random factor each time we update our Bayes' Inference Machine. In this model, the random factor is added to all updated probabilities without distinction to their authorization source origin, and including elements that, by model and process, were heretofore determined to be zero.

Thus,

$$R_{11}^{1}(t) = \frac{P(D/R_{11})R_{11}}{P(D)} + \sigma(t) \quad \textbf{(7-22)}$$

$$R_{12}^{1}(t) = R_{21}^{1}(t) = R_{22}^{1}(t) = \sigma(t) \quad \textbf{(7-23)}$$

Where $R_{11}^{1}(t)$ is the first Bayes correction term, etc.

The random element $\sigma(t)$ is time dependent, meaning its value changes each time we make a Bayesian correction depicted in Equation (7-22). Once we include the random element to example in Equation (7-16), we find

$$User\ Assertions = A(x_l, t) = \left[\begin{bmatrix} R_{11}^{1} & 0 \\ 0 & 0 \end{bmatrix} + \sigma(t).I\right]\begin{bmatrix} 1 & 0 \\ 0 & 1 \end{bmatrix} x_l \qquad \textbf{(7-24)}$$

Subsequent Bayes corrections would work as before, excluding the random factor in the correction, but adding it after the fact, for example:

If,

$$R'_{11} = \frac{P(D/R_{11})R_{11}}{P(D)} \qquad \textbf{(7-25)}$$

$$R''_{11} = \frac{P(D/R'_{11})R'_{11}}{P(D)} \qquad \textbf{(7-26)}$$

$$R'''_{11} = \frac{P(D/R''_{11})R''_{11}}{P(D)} \qquad \textbf{(7-27)}$$

etc., then,

$$R_{11}^{1}(t) = \frac{P(D/R_{11})R_{11}}{P(D)} + \sigma(T = t) \tag{7-28}$$

is the first Bayes correction term from above, and

$$R_{11}^{2}(t) = \frac{P(D/R_{11}^{1})R_{11}^{1}}{P(D)} + \sigma(T = t + \Delta t) \tag{7-29}$$

and

$$R_{11}^{3}(t) = \frac{P(D/R_{11}^{2})R_{11}^{2}}{P(D)} + \sigma(T = t + 2\Delta t) \tag{7-30}$$

etc., are subsequent correction terms, adjusted for the randomness factor described above.

§§

The final Risk Adjusted User Assertions is then given by

$$A' = \begin{bmatrix} R'_{11}(t)t_1r_1 & R''_{12}(t)t_1r_2 & \cdots & R'_{1n}(t)t_1r_n \\ R'_{21}(t)t_2r_1 & R'_{22}(t)t_2r_2 & \cdots & \cdots \\ \cdots & \cdots & \cdots & \\ & & R'_{ij}(t)t_ir_j & \cdots \\ R'_{m1}(t)t_mr_1 & R'_{m2}(t)t_mr_1 & \cdots & R'_{mn}(t)t_mr_n \end{bmatrix} \quad \textbf{(7-31)}$$

and each $R'_{ij}(t)$ is determined according to Equation (7-19) and the subsequent corrections based on the enterprise and industry evolution of that risk as captured by our model Equation (7-29) and Equation (7-30).

Propagation

So far, we have created a model for the authorization risk matrix post-authorizer, i.e. soon after the Assertion Matrix exits the authorizer. See below, Figure 7-3:

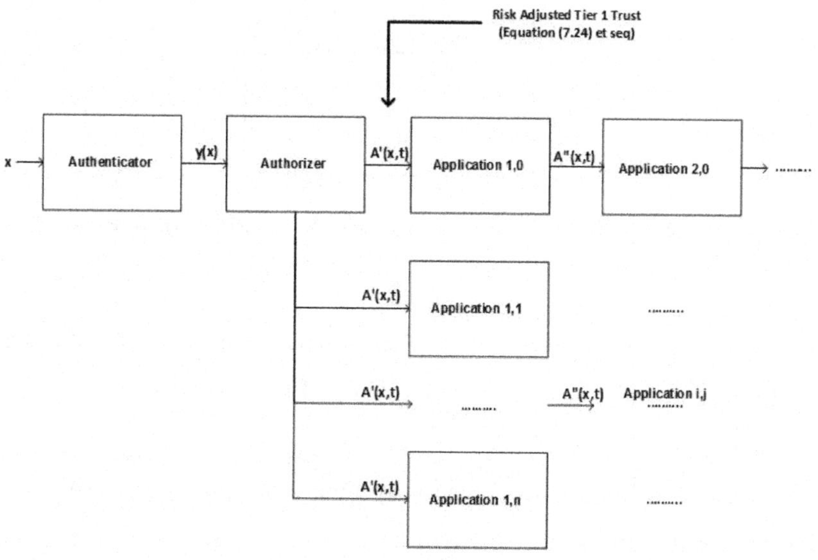

Figure 7-3: IAM Authorization Risk Propagation

Downstream applications which verify the received assertions with the authorizer will be un-affected by any intervening risks, except perhaps in cases where the comparison process itself is compromised. Thus, Figure 7-4:

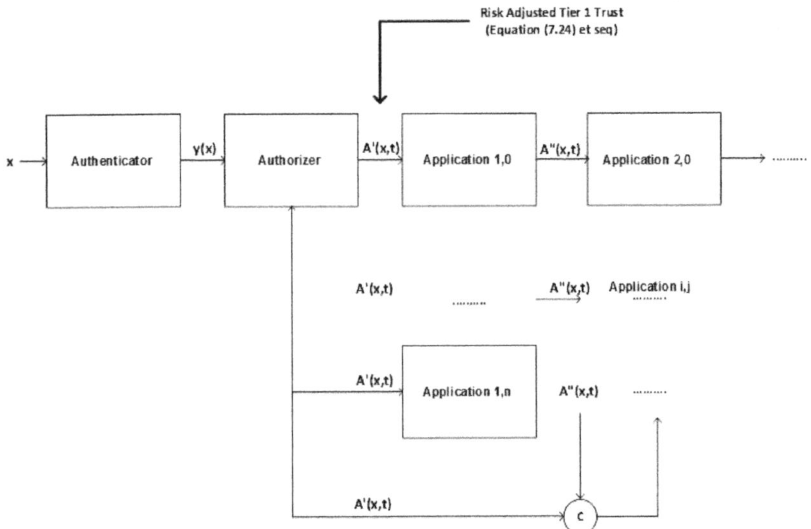

Figure 7-4: Application of a Downstream Assertion Comparator

The downstream assertion comparator (C) essentially ensures that the integrity of the assertions is unchanged from their source.

In cases where downstream applications do not verify the assertion explicitly according to Figure 7-4, that verification may be implicit in the trust implied by the shared secret used (or some such cryptographic check) to encrypt the assertion object.

SUMMARY

In this chapter, we have investigated and proposed several models that may be used to understand authorization mechanisms within an enterprise, taking into account internal and external factors.

In particular, we have posited a Bayesian approach to evolving authorization risk within the organization.

Chapter 8 – Functional IAM: Principles, Requirements, Processes, Policies and Standards

INTRODUCTION

In this chapter, we will switch gears and build the foundational principles of process-oriented IAM within the enterprise that use little or no mathematical formulation, but which help us think about the human aspects of IAM processes in the enterprise. We make the case for a unified approach to managing identities in a complex enterprise and discuss the models and framework for evolving such a unified approach using unified policies, processes and prescribe optimal organizational governance models to implement them.

We discuss the relationship with regulatory compliance, and other critical information enterprise functions. We also include non-prescriptive, strategic positions and models that organizations may take to streamline enterprise identity and access management.

ORGANIZING PRINCIPLES

This section provides an overview of high level organizing principles of an enterprise identity and access management infrastructure. It is organized into high level focus areas, roughly in order of strategic priority to the organization.

IAM Unification & Rationalization

Identity Management is the process of managing user identities (principals or 'users') in the enterprise. Traditionally, these include employees, contractors, business partners, supplies and vendors, amongst others. In the Services Oriented Architecture (SOA) world, identities may also be extended to business entities like assets, projects or web services.

The goal of Identity Management systems is to track user identities as they traverse through various phases in the enterprise. As the identities assume new roles, relinquish old ones, on-board and off-board, a properly designed Identity Management system manages the process seamlessly from one phase to the next.

Underlying each Identity Management system is an Access Management system. An Access Management system provides primarily authentication and authorization services, but may also provide other related services like non-repudiation. Once again, an Access Management system may provide services to traditional identities (principals or 'users') as well as non-traditional identities like servers and enterprise services.

These two services form the foundation of the enterprise information architecture. Their situation at the center of the information enterprise explains why they should occupy such a prominent mindshare of organizational leadership.

Control versus Management

A typical firm's Enterprise Information Architecture (EIA) evolves primarily from helter-skelter applications procurement standards, and through mergers and acquisitions.

In many of these organizations, each department acquires applications according to its needs, and each such application will introduce its own IAM services with little or no regard for existing centralized IAM services.

Of course mergers and acquisitions introduce disjointed systems and technologies even when the acquisition is within the same industry since the overriding determinant for a merger or acquisition is high level strategic business fit, not technology integration fit, with the latter being of third degree consideration, if at all.

Rationalizing disjointed technologies creates unique IAM challenges that every IAM leadership should address. At its core is the balance that must be struck between the application stakeholders' prerogative to control and manage their application according to their unique business needs, against the enterprise-wide enterprise information architecture rationalization goals.

While IAM and top leadership within the organization have an enterprise wide view of how the enterprise information architecture should look like, it is the application owners who must use IAM to meet every day business requirements. This puts the application owner in a position of strength when it comes to defining the parameters around the applications. It is also likely that the application owner is financially responsible for some portion of the IT budget, further enhancing their hand.

In these situations, IAM leadership (CISOs, CTOs and CIOs) may put into place application procurement standards and have it adopted at the highest levels of technology and executive management within the organization. Such procurement standards would set broad guidelines with a particular long term, rationalized enterprise architecture goal in mind. Any exceptions to the policy would then require the approval of a high level Enterprise Security Policy Board.

Enterprise Identity Stack Rationalization Strategies

A necessary first step towards a unified Identity and Access Management involves creating a clear *and* enterprise-wide understanding of managed identities. In all but the smallest organizations, this may be a daunting task since many firms typically grow via acquisitions. Each such acquisition adds a non-rationalized principal data to an often non-rationalized corporate identity stack.

Furthermore, even organizations that don't tend to evolve fairly complex business practices that filter into technology management.

Definition:

> ***Enterprise Identity Stack Rationalization*** *simply means that all enterprise principals and their interrelationships are uniquely identified within a firm's enterprise and its business ecosystem. Enterprise Identity Stack Rationalization calls for unique identification and attribution of all human and non-human identities – principals (users), servers, domain controllers, physical and non-physical assets, and web services.*

In practice, the previous definition implies, for example, that all applications recognize that the Windows Domain principal (user) "smith", as the same "Mr. Joe Smith" in the HR database, and that no collision exists between different data stores (e.g. Active Directory and HR system) attributions of this identity. It means that the entire enterprise application space is aware that Joe Smith from Acclaim Consulting Group, Inc in the vendor tracking system is not the same Joe Smith, also from Acclaim Consulting Group, Inc, in the sales automation system, who in turn, is not the same jsmith (consultant) in corporate LDAP.

It would seem like identity rationalization is a simple matter of reconciling user records from multiple sources, perhaps using some automated technology tool. This view, however, if far from accurate due to the process complexity tied to the gathering, storage and use of organizational identities.

A fair and strategic model recognizes that a large complex organization often consists of many disjointed systems, each with its own silo-ed Identity and Access Management repositories, access and control paradigms and ownership.

There is usually *some* limited application integration from an IAM perspective. Most applications in effect have most of the required IAM services built in. For example, the HR application has its own user repository, roles repository, authentication service, authorization service, identity management service, etc. The result is a hodge-podge IAM infrastructure where many data repositories, application services and functions are duplicated.

We depict this in Figure 8-1 below.

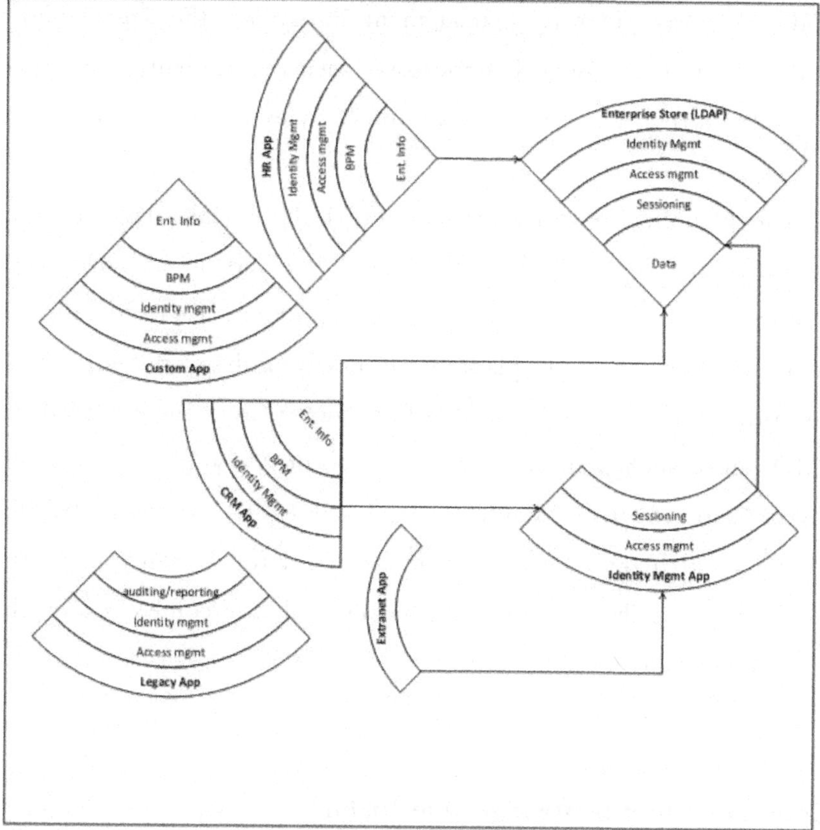

Figure 8-1: Non-Rationalized IAM Architecture

From this picture painted by Figure 8-1, we may develop a model that eases some of the process complexities that may be apparent from operating from such architecture.

Unify Corporate Identity Planning, Processes, and Leadership

Planning is a critical component of rationalizing the enterprise identity stack since identities span the entire organization plane and how the organization conducts its entire business. Therefore, before undertaking any identity management initiatives, the organization must put in place a plan that addresses identity rationalization from a business driver and core values points of view.

The planning must be carried out at the highest level of the enterprise (or the lowest level that has the ownership, authority and purview across the *entire* organization's interaction with its identities). In most cases, the only planning authority with proper view and corporate authority is a C-Level officer such a Chief Identity Officer (CIO) since such planning touches all corporate applications in all divisions of the firm. While the full scope of corporate Identity Management planning will take us far afield for present purposes, suffice it to say that the following elements should come out of such planning initiative:

Corporate Identity Management Vision

The C-Level officer may clearly enunciate an all-encompassing vision to not only create a direction that the entire organization may buy into and follow, but also articulate how identity management ties into the larger corporate goals like profitability, agility in execution of business plans and objectives (as we shall examine shortly), and other long term corporate goals.

A critical aspect of the corporate identity management vision is its evangelical aspect which empowers every member of the firm to be cognizant of appropriate aspects of corporate identity management. For example, it should be clear to the receptionist that phone calls should not be routed to an internal employee simply because the caller identified the employee by name or extension. This level of awareness is still widely lacking today just like it was for Mrs. Guerre in the 16th Century France (Chapter 3), and may only be blunted by widespread evangelization, not simply by an email reminder.

IAM Governance and Execution Strategy

Once the corporate Identity Management vision is articulated, a practical strategy for execution must be agreed upon. An execution model based on a promulgation of an organization-wide Identity and Access Management standing committee headed by the Chief Identity Officer (CIO) and drawing all application stakeholders, as the steering organ of all matters touching on corporate Identity and Access Management.

As an alternative model, a properly empowered existing standing committee may incorporate IAM governance functions. Regardless of its form, such a committee should not set strict guidelines for executing the organization's IAM vision; rather, driven by the corporate identity management and business imperatives, the committee should set an 80/20 execution strategy which we define as follows:

Definition:

> ***80/20 Execution Strategy*** – *Roughly 80 per cent of the corporate IAM strategy mandates should be relatively rigid, reflecting long term organization vision and core values, business imperatives and (as we shall see later on) aspects of governing regulatory regimes. 20 per cent of strategy mandates should remain relatively fluid to create departmental or organizational agility and empower lower level managers to use their own creativity to meet high level corporate Identity and Access Management vision at the time of execution. Note that there is no paradox from a regulatory perspective since virtually no regulatory mandates specifies implementation details, as we shall see shortly.*

Business Imperatives

Business imperatives supremely drive not just the vision but the execution strategy (and ultimately, the process model) of corporate identity management. For most organizations, the top three imperatives are business process efficiency, information security and, as much as possible, automated regulatory compliance. It is crucial that the planning phase bring out other imperatives that may be important to the firm and make all of them part of the corporate Identity and Access Management vision statement.

Enterprise Wide Application Procurement and Development Standards

In the error of information driven economies, it is a natural evolution that organizations will acquire many technologies and applications through departmental procurement processes as well as through mergers and acquisitions. Systems so acquired will create a cacophony of standards, technologies and infrastructure choices within the enterprise.

While this problem is intrinsic to business, firms can yet put in place processes and procedures to ensure that current systems are well integrated into a desired IAM framework and the new ones fit in with little or moderate integration effort.

The CIO may put in place enterprise-wide application procurement standards - or IAM-specific mandates added to the existing ones - that would, among other things:

- Set standards for selecting software vendors based on a enterprise wide criteria that outline how well they integrate within the organization's information infrastructure (i.e. "IAM fit" would be one criterion)

- Add "IAM fit" to the enterprise software development and integration standards. For example, require application developers and integrators to use existing enterprise IAM services instead of creating new ones within the application code.

- Set exception guidelines for business cases that dictate application solutions which fall outside of the firm's corporate procurement and software development standards, and following the prescribed 80/20 strategy.

Ideally, these standards would be adopted by the organization's management in charge of technology services so that all application owners have a clear controlling authority within which to operate.

Identity Data Rationalization

Identity Data Rationalization is part of the overall Enterprise Identity Rationalization and deals with the technical rationalization of user identities. In a very large financial institution, the task may be daunting given that the business ecosystem encompasses millions of user and non-user identities.

The best approach creates a Globally Unique IDentifier (GUID) for each identity across the enterprise. The actual creation of the GUID is quite easy using any number of GUID generation tools. The real challenge is assigning the GUID to the managed identities. Indeed, many IAM initiatives fail either because the identity data rationalization was not done properly or it takes so long to accomplish that it sucks time and budget off other Identity and Access Management project activities.

The best process model uses automated methods, say using some scripting facility, to uniquely identify principals followed by a manual process for principals that may not be identified automatically. It is critical to use heuristic matching methods with extreme restrain. For example, any automated method that tries to correlate the full name or some other such attribute heuristically across multiple user repositories is necessarily suspect unless it is accompanied by a massive manual check since it is susceptible to user data entry errors. On the other hand, a match based on a set of frequently used attributes creates a much more predictable automated match even if the methodology only covers a modest portion of the identity population.

Note on Standardized Directory Services

Directory Services are at the heart of the IAM enterprise information architecture. Establishing and standardizing directory services architecture is a critical step towards securing a unified IAM infrastructure since the directory services provide an excellent platform for aggregating access rights, storing identities and security policies, among others. Directory services enable other enterprise processes, including:

- *Identity and Access Provisioning*

- *Enhanced evolution of security policies and processes (auditing of application access, regulatory compliance, etc) which are easier done with a centralized enterprise directory services – see next section.*

Identity Data Mastering Models

Identity Data Mastering is another enterprise process that is easy to understand in theory but quite challenging to implement in practice, especially in complex organizations (which is most organizations).

Definition:

> ***Identity Data Mastering*** *simply refers to the designation of one or more enterprise systems as authorities for identity information. The simplest data mastering model designates a single system as the authoritative source of all identity data. In practice, however, large organizations normally have multiple data masters, with each one mastering specific attributes.*

The multiple data mastering model is more complex to implement, and in our view, makes it a lot harder to create a unified IAM regime, especially in situations where the number of data masters is beyond a handful. A multiple data mastering implementation is actually a harbinger for lack of executive IAM leadership or planning within an enterprise. It indicates that each division or department "clings to their data" against "encroachment" by others, usually, the information security department, and shows that there is no unified enterprise wide leadership envelope or model regarding Identity and Access Management.

A single data mastering approach designates a particular optimized system as the data master for all identity information. Any system that has any doubts about the quality of its identity data consults the identity master and updates its copy accordingly – see the following section on Provisioning.

A single identity data mastering model which unifies identity data across the enterprise, will greatly simplifies the enterprise Identity and Access Management systems implementation, but comes at some level of process and financial cost.

Identity Data Provisioning

The challenge of Identity Data Provisioning (also known as E-Provisioning) is to ensure that all enterprise identity and access data is kept in sync across all enterprise identity and access repositories and applications.

In many organizations, significant employee turnover, role changes, mergers and acquisitions, and divestitures make it very difficult to track identity information changes across multiple enterprise systems.

Identity and Access Provisioning drives employee productivity by enabling a new employee to begin performing her duties on the day they are hired or very close to it. Without a provisioning system, the new employees often wait for weeks to gain full access to all systems that they need to be productive.

Identity and Access Provisioning systems also come in handy when an employee leaves the firm's employment. When properly designed, such a provisioning system removes all rights from all systems on the day the employee leaves (or when the firm decides to terminate him). In many cases, organizations typically simply disable the employee's obvious access points (security badge, email and HR), but often leave a bevy of other accounts still active within the enterprise – UNIX-based accounts are notorious in this regard. These orphan accounts may be used by malicious actors, both internal and external, for activities that are not in the firm's best interest.

Firms also have a further reason to move to a streamlined Identity and Access Provisioning solution since many homegrown provisioning systems currently are limited in their capabilities and usually have substantial operational and maintenance costs.

Unfortunately, the provisioning solutions tend to be more complex to implement for technological and process reasons. A successful completion of enterprise leadership and planning is a pre-requisite of any provisioning initiative. In general, a good model implements the identity management and the provisioning solutions from the same software vendor since the two services are closely related.

Unified Access Management

Unified Access Management is closely linked to Unified Identity Management as we have discussed above, and indeed the two are often referred to in tandem as Identity and Access Management (IAM). At its core, Access management is supported by two key enterprise services, namely, Authentication and Authorization of identities to applications and enterprise services.

Just like identity management, access management requires high level enterprise-wide process planning. In fact, planning and overall execution of access management should go hand in hand with that of identity management. We highlight some of the differences that should be borne in mind in the following sections.

Unified Access Management Strategies

The concept of unifying the processes and systems used for enterprise application access management comes naturally to many organizations in the era of an information driven world. Access management often takes the form of IAM middleware vendor standardization and specialization, with IT managers arguing that developing vendor neutral Access Management models tend to be costly and unpredictable.

A better model, however, involves separating access management data from vendor implementation, leading to a degree of implementation/vendor independence. The idea is to be able to plug-in and out particular authentication and authorization service implementations that meet desired performance and scalability without changing the overall access management architecture.

The industry is clearly heading this way with recent innovations in Service Oriented Architectures (SOA), and as such any tight coupling of applications to authentication services implementations only serves to foreclose opportunities, especially for organizations where technological innovations power competitiveness. Instead, a best of breed model that picks and chooses vendors according to specific metrics is the best path to achieving the optimal IAM implementation.

Roles Based Access Management (RBAM)

Roles Based Access Management (RABM) creates an abstraction layer between application access management requirements – which may be expressed in very general business terms – and authorization implementation which is necessarily proprietary. A "Role" is a logical construct that represents the policy governing a principal's resource, application or service privileges.

In practice, the governing policy is invoked from business requirements (for example, "the HR application should only be accessed by HR managers") and is expressed in purely non-technical terms. A role is a logical representation of corporate policy, and ultimately relies on data managed by the Identity Management system (for example, "HR Role is assigned to principals in the HR department with title=Manager").

Note:

The role information is corporate data that resides in the data layer. The process of mapping roles to actors - Role Rationalization - can be quite complex and may bring out uncomfortable revelations, namely, that many organizations may not fully understand how they conduct their business – at least from the Identity and Access Management view point.

However, just like Identity Data Rationalization, Role Rationalization is a critical exercise during the building of a secure IAM infrastructure that also conforms to various regulatory regimes that mandate duty separation, and specific controls and audit provisions. Lastly, it is critical that Role Rationalization is performed in a completely IAM vendor neutral manner, as the opposite model creates artificial efficiencies that, while real, are linked to a vendor or technology choice that is not strategic to the organization's IAM vision and other imperatives mentioned above.

From the foregoing, it is apparent that unified access management is built upon, and is greatly facilitated by a unified identity data.

Unified Policy Evolution, Enforcement and Regulatory Compliance

Organizations evolve elaborate business driven security policies that ultimately must be enforced partly by IAM systems and other quasi-automatic technology driven systems. The other enforcement responsibilities are laid upon people, policy, processes and procedures.

Such security policies can be quite complex for a large number of organizations, especially given that multiple, often conflicting, requirements, must be met:

- Different stakeholders within a large enterprise may have conflicting security requirements. Even in cases where a single corporate office has executive authority over corporate security policies as we proposed in our earlier model, managing stakeholders, especially those from semi-autonomous departments, may be challenging.

- Business partners, for example, in the automated payment processing industry, may impose rigid security policies on its partners. Furthermore, the business side of the firm will be reluctant to foreclose business opportunities on account of insufficient IAM and other IT infrastructure.

- There are always constraints within a chosen technology, vendor and budget, and integration of multiple technologies/vendors for a best of breed solution has its own challenges and costs.

The above requirements may be met with one internal remedy or the other. Managing difficult stakeholders, for example, only requires sufficiently empowered and skilled leadership – many organizations, including the public sector, are not democracies, especially those in the competitive for-profit sectors. It is important that once a strategic organization direction and vision have been identified and proper leadership put in place, all stakeholders will conform accordingly or the organization will find new ones who will.

Even relationships with business partners may be managed accordingly especially in an environment of shared business goals and values regarding organization management.

IAM Models for Regulatory Compliance

The forgoing may not be said of regulatory compliance. Once promulgated, governmental mandates are normally set in stone for extended periods of time and non-compliance invites potentially very severe sanctions. Because of its huge impact on the design, implementation and operation of IAM systems, we devote the rest of this section to a discussion of IAM issues surrounding regulatory compliance.

Most organizations face multiple different laws and jurisdictions, regulations and industry standards worldwide when it comes to

Identity and Access Management. Given the global nature of many organizations today, a medium sized financial services firm in the USA, for example, will often find itself subject not only to out-of-state regulations like California's Information Practices Act but also overseas regulations like Hong Kong's Personal Data Privacy Act or Canada's Chapter P-21 Regulation.

The following table shows some of these regulations and a summary of what each entails (Williams 2005):

Regulation	***Authority***	***Type of Act***	***Summary***
Basel II — Revised International Capital Framework	*EU*	*Identifying, assessing, measuring, and controlling operational risks*	• *Takes a three-pillar approach to improve capital adequacy for large banks within the group of 10 nations. One pillar focuses on internal controls, and calls for review of control structures and risk management in order to ensure prudent conduct of business.* • *Sections 751 and 752 call for assessment of the control environment including the quality of information reporting and underlying systems.*
Gramm-Leach-Bliley Financial Services	*USA*	*Data privacy*	• *Allowed greater competition among banks, securities companies, and insurance companies, and allows*

Modernization Act			*investment and commercial banks to consolidate.* • *Requires financial institutions to provide each consumer with a privacy notice at the time the consumer relationship is established and annually thereafter. Consumers have the right to opt-out in order to limit some, but not all, sharing of information.*
Sarbanes-Oxley Act *(Sarbox)*	*USA*	*Disclosure and* *reporting*	• *Goal is to protect investors by improving the accuracy and reliability of corporate disclosures.* • *Requires each company to conduct an internal audit and make an annual statement about the effectiveness of internal controls, including IT controls. Controls also verified by external auditor.*
California Information *Practices Act* *SB1386*	*California*	*Data Privacy*	• *Requires companies and government agencies that store personal information on California residents to disclose any breach of security to those individuals affected.* • *It requires businesses to inform residents if their*

			unencrypted personal information — including name and either a driver's license number, Social Security number, or credit card or banking information — has been compromised.
European Union Data Privacy Directive (EUDPD)		*Data Privacy*	• *Establishes a Europe-wide set of legal principles for privacy protection to be enacted in all EU member states.* • *Prohibits the transfer of personal data from European Union countries to any countries that do not have "adequate" data protection laws.*
Health Insurance Portability and Accountability Act 1996 (HIPAA)	*USA*	*Personal health data portability and protection*	• *Protects health insurance coverage for workers and their families when they change or lose their jobs.* • *Requires the establishment of national standards for electronic healthcare transactions and national identifiers for providers, health insurance plans, and employers.*
Canadian Privacy Act,	*Canada*	*Data Privacy*	• *Extends current Canadian laws that protect the privacy of*

Chapter P-21			*individuals with respect to limited use of personal information held by organizations and that provide individuals with a right of access to that information.*
Hong Kong Personal Data Privacy Act	*Hong Kong*	*Data Privacy*	• *Protects the privacy of living individuals in relation to personal data.* • *Contributes to Hong Kong's continued economic wellbeing by safeguarding the free flow of personal data to Hong Kong from restrictions by countries that already have data protection laws.*
Management's Responsibility for Internal Control US OMB Circular A123			• *Imposes Sarbox-like regulations on all U.S. Federal agencies.* • *It is likely that state and local agencies will follow.*

These laws and regulations impose significant legal and financial penalties for non-compliance. As more information goes digital, it is only to be expected that the digital information protection and privacy regulations will only proliferate.

It is also significant to mention the potential loss of business or organization reputation due to adverse negative publicity that results from information security breaches. Corporate as well as individual customers are becoming increasingly aware of data security and privacy issues. Indeed, at the corporate level, many organizations should impose data security standards on their vendors and business partners, and impose severe business penalties for non-compliance, if only as an insurance against up-stream liability.

We outline some strategic models in the following sections to deal with an ever expanding list of rules, regulations and standards.

IAM Process Unification for Regulatory Compliance

It should be readily apparent that regulatory compliance is very much facilitated by a process/model of a unified identity and access management framework we have discussed above. This is because a great majority of the laws and regulations concern identity data privacy. In a unified identity and access management enterprise, safeguarding identities is greatly simplified for the simple reason that all identity data is tracked in one systematic process framework.

Furthermore, the other regulations dealing with disclosure, reporting and control are also easier to comply with in a unified process framework since there is a single source for all records regarding application access. Monitoring, information forensics and audit solutions fit right into the framework, raising the happy specter of automated compliance.

Another big advantage to unifying IAM systems and processes comes when externally mandated audits are required. The audits are simpler and more cost effective than in an enterprise where IAM functions are widespread and discreet since supplying information to compliance auditors may be accomplished by querying one (or a handful) of databases. Compliance auditors can also be assured that the supplied information is consistent once collection systems are verified.

Exploit Regulatory Commonalities

Organizations may choose to seek IAM solutions that exploit commonalities between the different regulations. A cursory glance at the above table, for example, indicates that the regulations fall into the broad categories of data privacy, process controls (or both), and risk management. A further rationalization will bring out other commonalities that may then be condensed into specific feature system functions, services, and processes.

It is also important to note that the investment in IAM systems should not achieve compliance as the primary benefit. Such a model often indicates that the organization's leadership and processes have failed to fully internalize and integrate the regulatory mandates into its business or organizational model, vision and core values. Data privacy, for example, is a mandate driven by consumers concerned about the privacy of their data and as such, compliance should be internalized into the organization's business model, especially since it applies to other types of information like the organization's intellectual or other proprietary information.

80/20 Execution Model Applied to Regulations

Most IAM-centric regulations and standards do not impose specific systems solutions; rather, broad as well as detailed regulatory goals are spelt out. It is thus possible to maintain model flexibility without compromising compliance. In thinking about regulatory compliance, therefore, organizations are better served by rationalizing the regulatory landscape into 80% firm guidelines while permitting flexibility for the remainder to allow line managers and integrators some implementation agility. Doing so not only promotes operational agility at the enterprise level, but also makes it more likely that the firm will meet its deployment schedules – a straightjacket model to meeting all provisions in all regulations does not have a reasonable chance of success.

Adopt a Controls Framework

Control Objectives for Information and Related Technology (COBIT) provides specific framework and governance guidelines specific to information technology. Constructed by IT Governance Institute (ITGI), COBIT has been widely adopted by many organizations, especially large institutions, as a controls framework.

Implementing COBIT and other frameworks like COS, ISO 17799 and ITIL will greatly facilitate a organization's compliance with controls-based regulations since COBIT is designed specifically for a controls regime. Furthermore, implementing COBIT will also provide a lot of mileage towards privacy and other data-related regulations by creating system-based control processes (Williams, 2005 & Kelley, 2006).

Additional Enterprise Services Related to IAM

The following sections summarize other enterprise services that enable or are enabled by a unified identity and access management model.

Unified Business Process Alignment

The power of Business Process Management is un-leashed when its principals (users, servers, and services) all have a unified view of each other and of the applications. In this scenario, a workflow process in HR application creates connections to all entities it needs to complete its business task without any un-intended manual intervention.

One business process function that is closely married with identity and access management, and which organizations cannot ignore is the previously discussed E-Provisioning. E-Provisioning ensures that the on-boarding of new employees is quick and that employee productivity is employed from day one. E-Provisioning also ensures that the off-boarding process is quick and painless for the firm. E-Provisioning further reduces identity theft vulnerability by eliminating zombie accounts that may be hijacked by internal employees and external malicious actors.

Additionally, E-Provisioning facilitates and enables other IAM and enterprise Information Security functions like RBAM, Security Audits and others. Lastly E-Provisioning enables regulatory compliance by facilitating a controls regime (for example, making sure that a corporation does not continue to pay an employee after he has been terminated)

From a Return on Security Investment (ROSI) and strategic perspectives, enterprise E-Provisioning is a "no brainer". Unfortunately, E-Provisioning projects will most likely tend to be complex, time consuming and involve a healthy degree of custom development for all but the simplest of IT enterprises.

Within a unified business process context, business automation and outsourcing become well defined, modular, efficient and in regulatory compliance, and business services like partner management become completely pluggable.

Unified Business Intelligence (BI) View

Business Intelligence (BI) is the process of managing and mining business information. BI services include Auditing, Reporting, Data Mining and Warehousing, among others.

Business Intelligence is built partially on top of the IAM services and provides critical business decision information at the hands of key decision makers of the firm, line of business or division within an organization. In order to deliver the most accurate business intelligence, a unified view of the information enterprise is normally a necessary pre-requisite.

Unified Application Management

Enterprise applications enable productivity and are becoming exclusive windows to the enterprise. On the other hand, enterprise entities (users, servers, services, business partners and even remote business services) require properly construed rights before gaining access to these applications to perform a business task.

A unified IAM enables a unified application management model whereby an identity is given the complete picture of the enterprise without hassle, challenge or security lapses that is common with most enterprise information architectures today.

Unified Enterprise Correspondence

Enterprise messaging has become almost synonymous with enterprise email in recent years as email has become a dominant form of electronic communication. To avoid this false analogue, we use an all-encompassing term *'correspondence'* to denote all forms of inter-communication between various principals within the enterprise, including its broader business network.

The actors in this inter-communication are obviously the principals – users, servers and services. A unified view of the principals obviously super-charges, simplifies, and re-casts the enterprise correspondence to an even more powerful role within the enterprise.

We condense and summarize the foregoing unified information architecture in Figure 8-2.

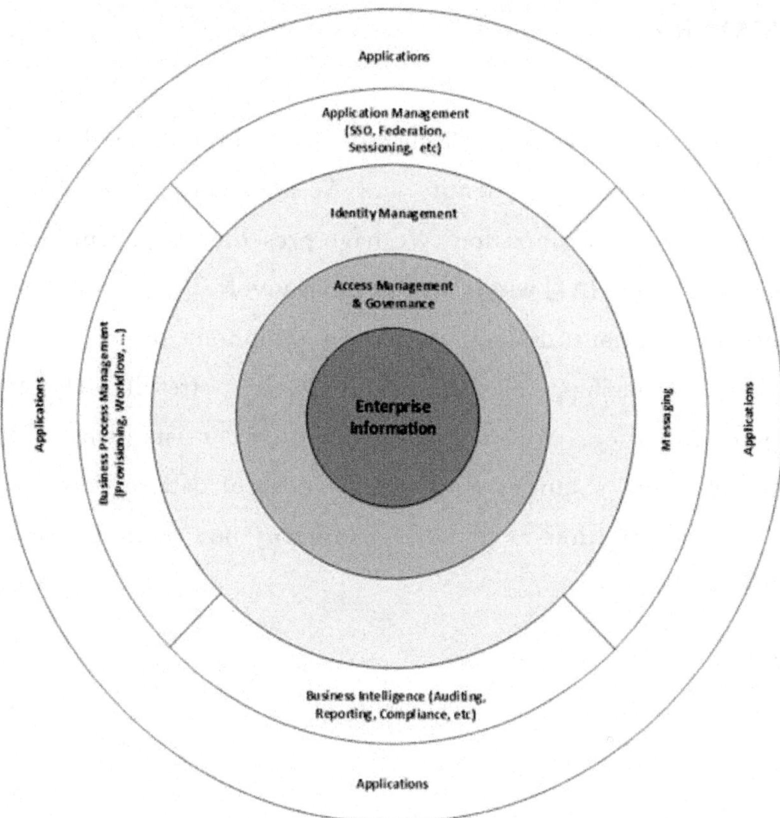

Figure 8-2: Enterprise Information Architecture: Unified IAM View.

SUMMARY

In this chapter, we have discussed several process models for efficiently implementing Identity and Access Management (IAM) within a complex organization. We have presented arguments that show that unifying IAM within an enterprise involves a lot more than technology solutions. Rather, it takes a symphony of high level corporate leadership, planning, and lastly, carefully chosen technology solutions. We present a model that consists of best-of-breed technology solutions with a heavy dose of data, system and process rationalization as the most efficient one from a whole process perspective.

Chapter 9 - Models of IAM Requirements, Policies, Processes and Standards

INTRODUCTION

Chapter 8 presented IAM as an interaction between technology, people and processes (presented as organizational processes, rules and regulations) to achieve "core organizational goals" and other business or organizational objectives.

Obviously the processes discussed are very human, with terms like "leadership", "rules", "regulations", "standards", "processes", and "organization's goals", many of which may not be measurable nor are they designed to be measured. Given this nature of IAM Processes, it is thus not amenable to a physical science like Engineering, but rather may be understood in the context of a social science.

For example, how a CISO cultivates, evolves and articulates an IAM Vision that the entire organization then follows, plus distinguishing why some organizations succeed in their IAM initiatives while others falter under apparently similar (measurable) factors may be left as a question to be answered by social science, along with questions to do with mood, perception and the like.

There are however aspects of IAM process within the organization that may be understood fairly well using Engineering concepts. Processes, for example, may be thought about as Rules and Regulations or Boundaries Conditions in Engineering terms. That is where we begin this short chapter, next.

BOUNDARY CONDITIONS

Suppose that a user has authenticated to the IAM system. According to our model from Chapter 2, Equation (2-22), the result of such authentication is given by

$$y[n] = \sum_{m=0}^{m=n} \vec{a}_l * \vec{b}_n * \delta[l-m] * \delta[m] \tag{9-1}$$

As you recall, Equation (9-1) simply states, almost literally, that "*Pick for me the right User ID and Password from the user repository.*"

According to Chapter 8, however, authentication is a lot more complicated since it may only happen within an *organizational process* framework. In other words, Equation (9-1) is only marginally true since it only captures the mechanics of authentication. Specifically, Equation (9-1) does not tell us anything about the organization where the authentication occurred (nor should it – in Chapter 2, we needed to build a generalized model that may be applied to *any* organization).

> *Equation (9-1) becomes completely true (or completely characterized) if we add the organizational context. In other words, we need to include the business requirements, standards, processes, rules and regulations that govern user authentication within the specific organization.*

But how do we think of organization process in the context of Equation (9-1)?

One model would be to treat business processes and government regulations as boundaries beyond which Equation (9-1) is no longer true. Thus we may write it as:

$$y[n] = \sum_{m=0}^{m=n} \vec{a}_l * \vec{b}_n * \delta[l-m] * \delta[m] \Bigg|_{f_1(\dots)f_2(\dots),\dots,f_n(\dots)} \qquad \textbf{(9-2)}$$

In Equation (9-2), $f_1(\dots)f_2(\dots),\dots,f_n(\dots)$ are all the non-trivial business requirements, rules, standards and regulations that govern the authentication process, and that are assumed to be "*out of process*" to the authentication context. For example, a rule stating that the user must have changed their password in the last 180 days before

Equation (9-1) returns a positive result upon the presentation of valid credentials may be considered in-process since that information is part of the authentication process. However, an organizational rule mandating that external users must not be logically mixed with internal users in the same user store is out-of-process, for example, if the user type is not part of the user record. Equation (9-2) would then contain all such out of process organizational policies and processes (and external government regulations) that have an authentication 'nexus' via $f_1(\ldots)f_2(\ldots), \ldots, f_n(\ldots)$.

From a model perspective, thus, one can imagine us grouping policies into different "*policy spaces*", with each policy space containing all organizational requirements, policies, rules, standards and government regulations affecting a particular IAM function, process or group of processes. One such policy space may govern User Authentication while another may govern roles assignment while yet another may govern user sessioning.

We can assume that these Policy Spaces will intersect in practice, and may represent them pictorially as follows, Figure 9-1:

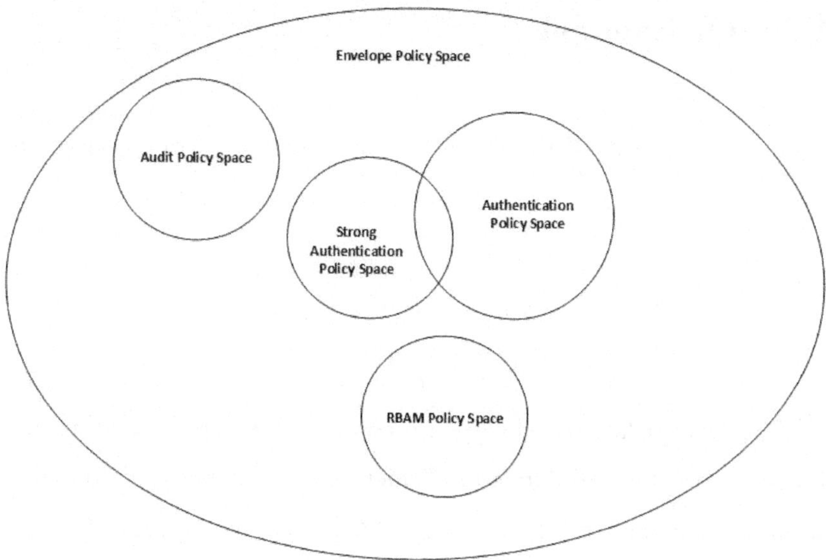

Figure 9-1: Pictorial Depiction of Policy Spaces

If we denote each policy space aρ_{AUTH}s, ρ_{SAUTH} , for example, we may re-write Equation (9-2) more precisely as

$$y[n] = \sum_{m=0}^{m=n} \vec{a}_l \vec{b}_n \delta[l-m]\delta[m] \Bigg|_{\{f_1(\dots) f_2(\dots),\dots,f_n(\dots)\} \in \{\rho_{AUTH}, \rho_{SAUTH}\}} \qquad \textbf{(9-3)}$$

Equation (9-3) simply means that the authentication has to satisfy organizational policies in the two policy spaces ρ_{AUTH}, ρ_{SAUTH}, which represent the authentication policy space and strong authentication policy space in Figure 9-1.

Equation (9-3), while a true conceptual device, does not point us to how we may use it in practice. We tackle this deficiency next.

A Simple Example

Imagine an organization that has the following policy regarding User Sessions:

The User Sessions are limited to 60 minutes.

We may translate this policy into concrete terms by imagining one dimension of the Authentication Policy Space to consist of a timeline running from some $t = t_0$ to $t = t_0 + 3600$ seconds, Figure 9-2.

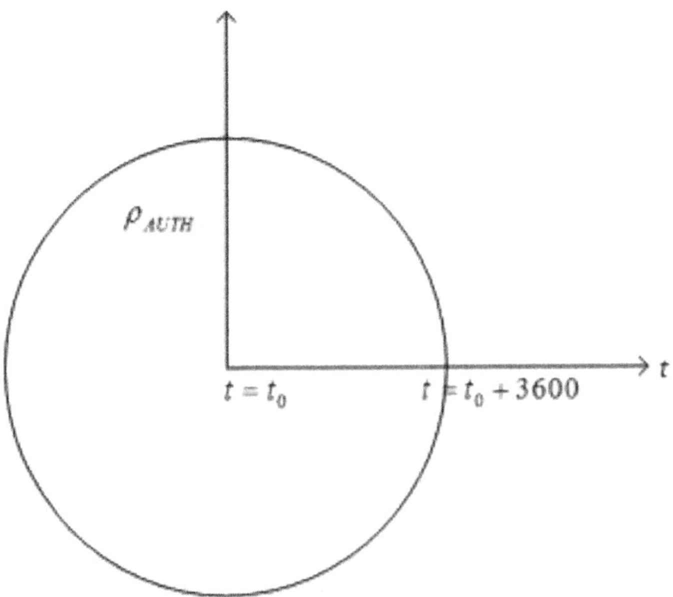

Figure 9-2: Authentication Space User Session Example

In, Figure 9-2 the user session conceptually starts at the center where $t = t_0$ and runs until the space boundary beyond which it must vanish.

Using elementary calculus, we may express this policy regarding user sessions as

$$f_1(t) = \int k(t)dt \quad \textbf{(9-4)}$$

which is simply a time integral/addition of some function $k(t)$ whose form we will determine precisely later.

The value of $k(t)$ is determined by the policy and per the stated user sessions policy, it is enough for $k(t)$ to be constant at all times before 60 minutes (3600 seconds) within the Authentication Space and vanish thereafter:

$$k(t) = \begin{cases} k, t < 3600 \\ 0, t \geq 3600 \end{cases} \quad \textbf{(9-5)}$$

We may combine Equations (9-3)-(9-5) in a straightforward manner to create the boundary condition for the user session policy, namely:

$$\int_{t_0}^{t_0+t} k(t')y[n]dt' = 3600 \quad \textbf{(9-6)}$$

Equation (9-6), after an appropriate choice of the constant *k*, is the boundary condition that the authentication depicted in Equation (9-1) must satisfy for it to comply with the organization policy requirement that all user sessions not last more than 60 minutes (a user session is defined from the start of an authentication until the end of its validity).

One may argue that Equation (9-5), on which Equation (9-6) is based, is rather arbitrary and thus involves a sleight of hand analysis. Equation (9-6) is arbitrarily chosen since policies are often arbitrary and are specific to an organization, such that the goals on which a policy is based is beyond the reach of a generalized analysis. The point of this example, therefore, is to show that a framework exists to analyze an arbitrary policy - see next section.

GENERALIZED BOUNDARY CONDITIONS

In the previous section, we modeled a relatively simple boundary condition using one dimensional (time) variables stemming from a simply stated policy requirement. We derived two equations to describe the underlying operation (authentication) unconstrained by policy, and another that expresses the result of the first as a condition derived from the stated organizational policy.

While this is a very simple model, the underlying two equation system is indeed very general and captures the principles of even the most sophisticated operation and organizational policy.

Thus, for any organizational function that we can model, we may derive a constitutive relationship that describes how the functional model relates to other modeled parameters - for example Chapter 2, Equation (2-22) describes authentication, Chapter 3, Equation (3-39) for authorization, etc:

Constitutive Relationship:

$$F(\ldots) = G(\ldots) \qquad \textbf{(9-7)}$$

where $F(\ldots)$ is a function of the output variable(s) we are concerned about – see Chapter 2, Equation (2-22) for example, and $G(\ldots)$ is the same function expressed in terms of the input or dependent variables.

This constitutive relationship is then matched by a set of boundary conditions of the form:

Boundary Conditions:

$$\psi_1(F(\dots),\dots)=0$$

$$\psi_2(F(\dots),\dots)=0$$

(9-8)

$$\dots\ \dots\ \dots$$

$$\psi_n(F(\dots),\dots)=0$$

In general, we expect that there will be one constitutive relationship of the form of Equation (9-7), accompanied by a set of boundary conditions in the form or Equations (9-8), which are of the form of Equation (9-6) except we have moved all terms to the left of the equation.

The important thing to note is that Equation (9-7) is true in all policy space under consideration while each equation in Equations (9-8) is true only within a specific organizational policy space.

We may also consider a more general boundary condition suggested by Equations (9-8), which point us away from the simple one dimensional and closed construct of Figure 9-2. In real life, regulations rarely tend to be closed, rather, they consist of a 'rule regulation or policy surface' which may not be crossed. For example, we may imagine a textured mesh surface of arbitrary shape depicted below, Figure 9-3:

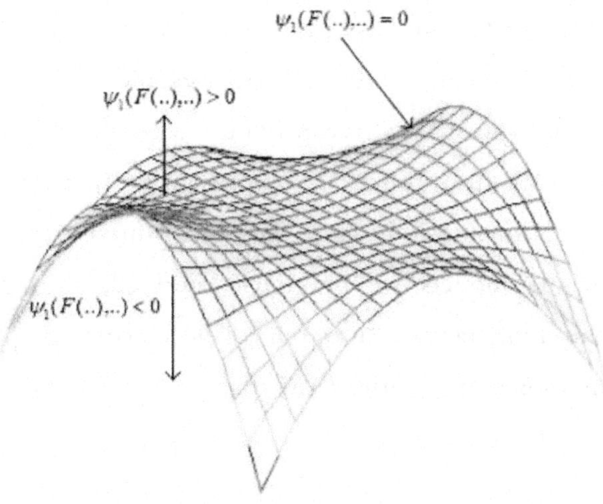

Figure 9-3: Example Policy Surface Depiction

As may be seen in Figure 9-3, all boundary conditions of Equation (9-8) must match at the policy boundary at once since policy mandates are often connected and we cannot simply break the individual rules into their own spaces as we depicted in the simple example above.

The difficulty of adhering to organization and governmental regulations is perhaps indicated by Figure 9-3, especially as we consider that the policy surface may be constantly changing with time (as new teams get into positions of management, new political regimes assume office, etc). In engineering terms, we have turned Equations (9-8) into a set of dynamic continuity relations.

SUMMARY

In this brief chapter, we have sketched a way to think about and model IAM Requirements, Policies, Processes and Standards within the organization. Specifically, we provided a Systems Engineering approach to model these functions by presenting them in terms of constitutive relationships. Lastly, the constitutive relations are connected to the models we previously derived, allowing us to include human type factors into our overall effort to provide a systems foundation to the entire IAM space.

Chapter 10 - Financial Models in Identity and Access Management

INTRODUCTION

We conclude this book with a simply applied model that describes how organizations may think about their financial investments in Identity and Access Management, thereby showing, hopefully, that complicated math is not required to create a solid model. Undoubtedly, this is a very big part of the IAM process since almost every technology or model choice will ultimately rest on whether the organization is willing to expend the resources necessary to bring it to fruition.

Most organizations would agree that securing their information assets is worth some investment. It is thus plausible to assume that low levels of IAM security investment indicate that only a small portion of the firm's business is IAM asset value driven. It could also point to a misunderstood or mis-modeled corporate investment policy.

Conversely, some firms may be investing more than is warranted given the value of their information asset holdings, thereby wasting shareholder resources. The question then becomes: What level of IAM security investment is enough, and is this a question we can answer using a relatively simple models?

Several models exist to help companies set their IAM spending in general and Information Security spending in particular. The leading model out there is the Information Technology Portfolio Management (ITPM) model. This is really a version of the financial portfolio management theory applied to the information technology realm. Thus ITPM tries to optimize IAM spending based on a number of factors like business value, efficiency and cost reduction among others. Despite current vigorous research at esteemed institutions like the Center for Information Systems Research (CISR) at MIT and at the Free University of Amsterdam, ITPM is still in its infancy and the field would benefit from alternative models.

In the following sections, using the same philosophy as the rest of the book, we build an alternative model of IAM security spending that organizations may readily apply when setting their IAM budgets. The model is analytical and starts by developing a model for the business value of information. It then develops a model for the cost of an information security breach. Finally, we find the relationship between the value model and the cost model from.

MODELING IAM SECURITY SPENDING

The first consideration for an organization when determining IAM investment level is obviously the value of the information being protected. If the value of the firm's information assets is relatively low, there is really no need to spend a large (or any) portion of it in IAM initiatives; the firm is better off investing its resources elsewhere.

Conversely, firms should consider an IAM investment level commensurate with how much those IAM assets drive sales or some other measure of business or organization value creation. This principle is not new; historically, for-profit organizations have used it to allocate marketing dollars by, for example, setting aside 5% of revenues to fund sales activities.

Let's call the firm's information asset value ***Va***.

In an information-based economy, it is reasonable to assume that ***Va*** has some relationship to some measurable company financials like total sales or revenues (for if such a relationship did not exist, then the firm should not be spending precious dollars to protect or manage its information assets). We will discuss the exact manner of dependence momentarily.

Note that as a practical matter, there will exist an IAM investment floor at any given firm. This is the so-called 'keep the lights on', or some otherwise minimum IAM spending required to be in the game. We are not particularly interested in this investment floor since we seek an optimal level that may be above or below it.

The second major consideration in determining a firm's IAM Investment is the cost to the firm of an information security breach. The cost of a breach aggregates several factors. These mainly consist of breach response costs, regulatory fines levied, the costs of defending and/or settling law suits, and the value of lost business, revenues, relationships, reputational loss, and goodwill.

Let's call the total cost to the firm of a breach ***Vc***.

Plausibly, ***Va*** and ***Vc*** are related. We will revisit this later.

In the following sections, we develop models for ***Va*** and ***Vc***.

INFORMATION ASSET VALUE (VA):

Of what value to an organization is information that needs protection? Again ignore the un-interesting "floor" investment and instead focus on the as yet unknown optimal IAM investment level.

At a glance this is a very difficult question to answer generally. However, it is a little bit easier to tackle by zeroing in on the business value of the information:

Model Basis:

An information asset is valuable to the firm solely because of the asset's ability to generate ***future*** *revenues and goodwill for the enterprise. Present or past value of the information asset is not of interest to the organization except in so far as it contributes to goodwill which the firm may capitalize on in the future.*

To arrive at the information asset value as it relates to future income generation, thus, we simply take the current sales or revenues of the firm, factor in the contribution from the information assets in question, and then capitalize it using the firm's 'multiple' – the ratio that the market applies to earnings of the firm - the firm's Price to Earnings (PE) ratio. If the firm is private, PE ratios for similar public firms or the firm's industry PE may be utilized. For non-profits or governmental entities, a similar for-profit organization PE or a similar for-profit sector PE may be used.

The factor of sales or revenues contributed by the information assets will obviously differ from one organization to another, but it should be fairly straightforward to determine in some cases, but perhaps not others.

We also need to subtract the investments needed to secure and otherwise 'enable' the information asset since we realize that information assets must be 'unlocked' before they can become valuable to the organization. The enablement is considered value added – for example, data sitting on a database somewhere within the firm is not really valuable until it is protected, mined and applied to marketing activities or used in a product offering.

It is critical however not to define enablement so widely as to be useless for the purposes of a model – for example, we should only include activities that make the information usable to the business to generate income. Such activities include IT functions like data/application protection, perhaps data mining and modeling, but should not include 'second order' activities like marketing or customer acquisition that only leverages information asset's value.

In short hand therefore, we may write

$$V_a = V_s - V_e \qquad \textbf{(10-1)}$$

whereby:

V_a = information asset value.

V_s = capitalized value of sales driven by the information asset.

V_e = information value added which includes IAM investments and related spending as above.

In the following sections, we provide two examples that illustrate the relationship between information asset value and IAM spending levels. We begin by using the well-known Coca Cola's secret ingredient. Note that these examples are for illustration purposes only.

Example 1: Coca Cola's Secret Ingredient:

The huge sales and global market dominance of Coca Cola's Coke soft drink are reasonably based in part on the firm's famous 100+ year old information asset, namely secret ingredient that makes the drink unique and popular amongst all competing carbonated drinks.

If you are the VP of Sales for Coca Cola, you could perhaps determine pretty accurately what portion of Coca Cola Company's overall $25B (mid 2000s) in sales came from Coke (A cursory investigation seems to indicate the fraction is a little over 55%).

We will assume Coke sales are 55% of Coca Cola's total sales of $25B or $14B.

It is probably also pretty easy to figure out the secret ingredient attribution to this sales figure.

We will assume the fraction is 25%.

Using these assumptions, the Information Asset value of Coca Cola's secret ingredient is about $250B (after factoring in an example forward PE of 18)

In this hypothetical Coca Cola scenario, and considering just the secret coke ingredient only,

$$V_a = 250 - V_e \ (in\ Billions\ \$) \quad \textbf{(10-2)}$$

Example2: TJX Companies

According to press accounts and company press release (TJX, 2007), sometime in early 2000s, an innovative but wholesomely criminal enterprise planted what may be described as a listening bug on TJX Company's systems and stole credit and debit card data for some staggering 45.7 million TJX customers!

The credit card information per se can and should be considered an information asset since, among other reasons, retailers long realized that swiping the card (as opposed to paying cash or writing a check) leads to increased sales. TJX may also leverage the credit card information in its marketing, further adding sales value above the 'credit card' effect.

Note that whether the credit card information was stored in TJX's systems or not does not matter to our model. It only matters that TJX had custody of the information for some duration of time.

Nonetheless, the factor of sales attributable to credit card information asset should be determinable – let's say the effect is 20%. With estimated sample sales of $17B and a PE of 17 and assuming ½ of all sales are done via credit or debit cards, the hypothetical TJX Companies scenario with regards to credit card information asset value is:

$$V_a = 29 - V_e \ (in\ Billions\ \$) \qquad \textbf{(10-3)}$$

FINDING A COST OF BREACH MODEL

The cost of an IAM security breach is relatively easy to estimate once a breach occurs. However, we are more interested in creating a model for estimating the cost of a potential breach, i.e. before one occurs.

To estimate potential costs of a security breach, we break it down to its main components for simplicity, namely economic losses by affected parties, regulatory payments and lost business. We discuss each in turn in the following sections.

Economic Losses in Affected Parties

Since the organization is most often a custodian, not the owner of information assets, the economic losses in affected parties deals with potential losses incurred by the proper owners of the data after a breach, including company shareholders. This may include losses suffered by credit card holders, the issuing banks or financial losses resulting from identity theft. It may also include loss in shareholder value from theft of trade secrets or intellectual property.

To estimate economic losses from an IAM security breach, we add up their entire capitalized value. For example, the economic loss resulting from a breach of credit card information is the sum of all unused balances (assumes that credit card companies enforce some kind of limit on each card). Presumably this is also the cost of defending and settling the inevitable law suits from a breach.

In the case of intellectual property theft, it is the reduction in shareholder value or organizational goodwill arising from the assets being used to hurt the its future revenues, sales, competitiveness and goodwill.

Similarly, the economic value of a lost identity may be determined based on the value of fraud that may be perpetrated using the stolen identities before the fraud is detected and stopped.

Alternatively, we may simply estimate the cost of defending and settling resulting customer, shareholder or citizen lawsuits. This approach may be accurate albeit Machiavellian and morally hazardous. For example, the organization may come to the conclusion that defending consumer lawsuits is cheaper that setting the proper IAM Spending Level necessary to prevent a breach.

Regulatory Penalties

The payments for regulatory penalties are normally spelt out in applicable laws (see Orondo, 2007), and may simply be added up.

Loss of Business

The Lost Business or Goodwill resulting from a breach is not easy to estimate or model. Empirical studies, for example, have shown that publicly traded companies lose an average of 25% in market capitalization for at least one year after an information asset breach. Empirical studies may however be misleading and hard to apply to any particular firm.

Instead of relying on empirical data, we have to go back to the value of the breached information to the business and estimate the extent of the potential business loss based on media publicity and Internet buzz.

Since we already have a basis for capitalized information asset value, the only missing component is what we may call the "business loss index" – the percentage of the firm's business or goodwill that is lost – and this can be 100% in some cases.

A key metric for determining the loss index is media saturation – note that even though several privacy regulations require client notification in case of information breaches, individual notifications have less impact than exposure to media.

To measure media impact, thus, a firm has to consider where the trigger points for the business loss are – for credit card losses, the trigger points may be consumers and potential customers choosing to shop at competitors' stores. These consumers will most likely watch the adverse news on the evening bulletins or read about it online, thus a metric or scale may be devised accordingly.

For a business-to-business relationship, the media saturation point will be business partners and the firm can safely assume the media saturation will be 100%; how much business is lost will be determined by other factors like ease of switching to competitor products or services, etc.

There are obviously other factors, but we can use the business loss index multiplied by the capitalized information asset value as the approximate value of lost business.

Putting everything together, the cost to a business of a security breach is indicated as:

$$V_c = L_e + R_p + L_i * V_a \qquad \textbf{(10-4)}$$

whereby:

V_c = cost of an information security breach

L_e = Economic loss of affected parties

R_p = Regulatory penalties

L_i = Business loss index

V_a = Value of information asset

Using Equation (10-1), we may write Equation (10-4) as:

$$V_c = L_e + R_p + L_i * (V_s - V_e) \quad \textbf{(10-5)}$$

where:

V_a = information asset value

V_s = capitalized value of sales driven by information asset

V_e = information value added which includes IAM spending.

Cost of Breach, Information Asset Value Relationship

The cost of an information security breach must be discounted by the likelihood of a successful breach occurring. As before, the simple insurance model seems appropriate for this case. In other words, the firm should invest no more than the modeled cost of the breach multiplied/reduced by the likelihood of the breach materializing.

If that likelihood or probability of a breach is labeled P_b, then the discounted cost, labeled V_d, is

$$V_d = P_b * V_c \qquad \textbf{(10-6)}$$

Using Equation (10-5),

$$V_d = P_b * \left(L_e + R_p + L_i * (V_s - V_e)\right) \qquad \textbf{(10-7)}$$

Using the insurance model, then, V_d is exactly the amount of investment that the firm should be willing to make in order to avoid paying a substantially higher cost, V_c – we have assumed that the fractional likelihood of a breach occurring is not close to certainty.

But V_d is exactly the Information Asset Value added, V_e, the amount of investment that the firm should be willing to make to safeguard its information assets.

Putting things together, we get the following:

$$V_e = P_b * \left(L_e + R_p + L_i * (V_s - V_e)\right) \quad \textbf{(10-8)}$$

Solving for V_e in Equation (10-8), we get

$$V_e = \frac{P_b}{1 + P_b L_i} * \left(L_e + R_p + L_i V_s\right) \quad \textbf{(10-9)}$$

Note that the likelihood of a breach given adequate information security resources, P_b, should be quite low, but not zero. Because the business loss index, L_i, is also a fractional quantity, we may simplify the above relationship, Equation (10-9), as follows:

$$V_e \cong P_b * \left(L_e + R_p + L_i V_s\right) \quad \textbf{(10-10)}$$

where:

V_e = The information asset value added which includes IT security spending

P_b = The likelihood of an information asset breach

L_e = The economic loss of affected parties resulting from information asset breach

R_p = The regulatory penalties from the information asset breach

L_i = Business loss index (based on breached information assets)

V_s = The capitalized value of sales driven by breached information assets

In this relationship, all factors are referenced to the same information assets.

This result is exactly what we would expect:

IAM investment or spending should be no more than the discounted value of any potential losses from breaches, plus the discounted value of the potential loss of value driven sales. This means that as the firm's sales get more dependent on information assets, more resources should be allocated to ensuring those assets don't fall into the wrong hands.

Conversely, as a firm's sales increasingly depend on IT, lack of commensurate information security investment is risk that your firm cannot afford to carry.

Note:

In practice, the above relationship, Equation (10-9), is not linear. Each component is related to other variable factors within the firm, thus, for example:

$$V_e(x, y, z, \ldots) \cong P_b(x) * \left(L_e(y) + R_p(z) + L_i(x, y) * V_s(x, y, z)\right) \qquad \textbf{(10-11)}$$

where:

$x, y, z, \ldots$ are the dependent parameters whose nature of dependence will vary from firm to firm.

SUMMARY

In this chapter, we have formulated an alternative framework model that may be easily used by firms to determine the level of IAM investment. Our model ties IAM investment to the business value generated by information assets being protected, and yields a result that is significantly simpler to understand and implement than those based on more complicated models like ITPM.

Chapter 11 - References

CHAPTER 1

Statistics Canada, "History of the Census" (Retrieved October 2016), *http://www.statcan.gc.ca/edu/power-pouvoir/ch2/history-histoire/5214912-eng.htm*.

Kuhrt, A., (1995), "The Ancient Near East c. 3000–330BC, Vol 2", *Routledge, London*, pp. 695.

Indian Census Bureau, Retrieved October 2016, http://www.censusindia.gov.in/

H. Yoon (1985). "An early Chinese idea of a dynamic environmental cycle", *GeoJournal* **10** (2), pp. 211-212.

Constitution of the United States, Article 1, Section 2.

Orondo, (2007), "Unified Identities in Complex Financial Organizations", *Managing Information Assurance in Financial Services*, pp. 190-207.

Lampson, B. W., (1974), "Protection", *ACM Operating System Review*, Vol 8, no 1, pp. 18-24.

Lampson, B. W., (1973), "A Note on Confinement Problem", *Communications of the ACM*, Vol 16, no. 10, pp. 613-615.

Chandra, A, Kozen, D and Stockmeyer, L, (1981), "Alternation", *J. ACM 28, 1, 114-133.*

Abadi, M, Burrows M, Lampson, B, and Plotkin, G, (1993), "A Calculus for Access Control in Distributed Systems", *ACM Transactions on Programming Languages and Systems*, Vol. 15, No. 3.

Rivest, R., A. Shamir, L. Adleman (1978), "A Method for Obtaining Digital Signatures and Public-Key Cryptosystems", *Communications of the ACM 21 (2): pp.120–126.*

Diffie, W., Hellman, M. (1976), "New directions in cryptography", *IEEE Transactions on Information Theory* 22 (6): 644–654.

Garey, M and Johnson, D (1979). "Computers and Intractability: A Guide to the Theory of NP-Completeness", *W.H. Freeman.*

Delfs, Hans and Knebl, Helmut (2007), "Symmetric-key encryption". *Introduction to Cryptography: Principles and Applications*, Springer.

Simmons, G, 1979, "Symmetric and Asymmetric Encryption", *Computing Surveys, Vol 11, No. 4.*

Benantar, M., 2006, "Access Control Systems, Security, Identity Management and Trust Models", *Springer*, pp. 9-10.

Ferraiolo, D., Barkely, J., & Kuhn, D, (1999), "A Role-based control model and reference implementation within a corporate intranet", *ACM Transactions on Information and System Security, 2 (1).*

Nyanchama, M, & Osborn, S, (1999), "The Role Graph Model and Conflict of Interest", *ACM Transactions on Information and System Security, 2 (1).*

Zhang, Z., Zhang, X., Sandhu, R., (2007), "Towards a Scalable Role and Organization based Access Control Model with Decentralized Security Administration", *Social and Organizational Liabilities in Information Security,* Gupta, M & Sharman, R., *eds.*

Azzedin, F, & Maheswaran, M., (2002), "Evolving and Managing Trust in Grid Computing Systems", *Proceedings of the 2002 IEEE Canadian on Electrical Computer Engineering.*

Grandison, T., Sloman, M., "A Survey of Trusts in Internet Applications", *IEEE Communications Surveys & Tutorials*, Vol. 3, No. 4, 2000.

Siebert, M., 1986, "Circuits, Signals and Systems", *MIT Press*, 1986

J. B. J. Fourier, 1822, "Theorie Analytique de la Chaleur".

de Santillana, G., 1961, "The Origins of Scientific Thought", 1961.

CHAPTER 2

Siebert, M., (1986), "Circuits, Signals and Systems", *MIT Press.*

Dirac, P., (1958), "Principles of quantum mechanics (4th ed.)", Oxford at the Clarendon Press.

Heaviside, O., (1892), "On Operators in Physical Mathematics, Part I", *Proceedings of the Royal of London, Vol. 52, 505-529.*

Heaviside, O., (1893), "On Operators in Physical Mathematics, Part II", *Proceedings of the Royal of London, Vol. 54, 105-143.*

Todorov, D, (2007), "Mechanics of User Identification and Authentication", *Auerbach Publications.*

CHAPTER 3

Orondo, (2007), "Unified Identities in Complex Financial Organizations", *Managing Information Assurance in Financial Services*, pp. 190-207, 2007.

Ferraiolo, D., Barkely, J., & Kuhn, D, (1999), "A Role-based control model and reference implementation within a corporate intranet", *ACM Transactions on Information and System Security, 2 (1).*

Nyanchama, M, & Osborn, S, (1999), "The Role Graph Model and

Conflict of Interest", *ACM Transactions on Information and System Security, 2 (1).*

Zhang, Z., Zhang, X., Sandhu, R., (2007), "Towards a Scalable Role and Organization based Access Control Model with Decentralized Security Administration", *Social and Organizational Liabilities in Information Security,* Gupta, M & Sharman, R., *Eds.*

Hoare, C., (1969), "An Axiomatic Basis for Computer Programming", *Communications of the ACM, Volume 12 Issue 10, 1969.*

Cantor et al., eds., (2005), "Assertions and Protocols for the OASIS Security Assertion Markup Language (SAML) V2.0", *OASIS*, *www.oasis-open.org*.

CHAPTER 4

Osmanoglu, E., 2013, "Identity and Access Management", *Elservier*, 2013.

CHAPTER 5

Davis, 1983, "The Return of Martin Guerre", *Harvard University Press*, 1983.

Finlay, 1988, "The Refashioning of Martin Guerre", *The American Historical Review*, Vol. 93, No. 3. (June 1988), pp. 553-571.

Eichenwald, K, 2000, "The Informant", *Broadway Books*, NY, 2000.

Luhmann, N, 1989, "Vertrauen. Ein Mechanismus der Reduktion sozialer Komplexität", *3d ed., Stuttgart, Enke.*

Denning, P. J., Metcalfe R. M., 1997, "Beyond Calculation. The Next Fifty Years of Computing", *Copernicus.*

Bernstein, P, 1998, "Against The Gods: The Remarkable Story of Risk", *John Wiley & Sons,* pp. 116.

CHAPTER 7

Orondo, P, 2008, "An Alternative Model of Information Security Investment", Social and Organizational Liabilities in Information Security, pp. 133-140, *Information Science Reference, IGI Global.*

Mukhopadhyay, et al, 2008, "E-Risk Insurance Product Design", Social and Organizational Liabilities in Information Security, pp. 133-140, *Information Science Reference, IGI Global.*

CHAPTER 8

Kelley, D (2006), "Become Compliant Without Breaking the Bank", *Information Security, 28.*

"The HP Identity Management Journey: Identifying an Effective Solution", August 2005.

"The Value of Identity Management", http://www.pwcglobal.com, 2002.

TJX, "The TJX Companies, Inc. Victimized by Computer Systems Intrusion; Provides Information to Help Protect Customers" (Retrieved October 2016), http://investor.tjx.com/phoenix.zhtml?c=118215&p=irol-newsArticle&ID=951253&highlight=.

Williams, C. (2005) "Leveraging Regulatory Compliance Investments to Add Business Value", *BMC Software, Inc Business Practices White Paper*, 2.

CHAPTER 9

Bartels, A (2007), "IT Spending and Forecasting", *Forrester Research*.

Symons, C, (2005), "Optimizing the IT Portfolio for Maximum Business Value", *Forrester Research*.

Markowitz, H. (1952), "Portfolio Selection", *Journal of Finance*, 7 (1), 77-91.

Orondo, P. (2007) "Unified Identities in Complex Financial Organizations", *Managing Information Assurance in Financial Services*, Rao et al (Editors), 190-207.

Chapter 12 - Index

Made in the USA
Middletown, DE
09 August 2021

45691446R00189